For Sr. Margaret Mary Anne savor — a colleague, friend and luncheon companion -- as well as for God, Country and Podoria.

Frank Redmond wg
2/24/87

*For God,
Country, and Polonia*

For God, Country, and Polonia:

One Hundred Years of the Orchard Lake Schools

Frank Renkiewicz

Center for Polish Studies and Culture
Orchard Lake Schools/Orchard Lake, Michigan

Copyright ©1985 by SS. Cyril and Methodius Seminary,
St. Mary's College, St. Mary's High School

All rights reserved

SS. Cyril and Methodius Seminary,
St. Mary's College, St. Mary's High School
3535 Indian Trail
Orchard Lake, Michigan 48033

Library of Congress Catalog Card Number: 85-72080

ISBN: 0-9615564-0-4

Printed by Harlo Press, 50 Victor, Detroit, Michigan 48203

CONTENTS

	Foreword	7
	Preface	9
I.	The Source	13
II.	The Polish Seminary	21
III.	The Polish American Seminary, 1909-1942	59
IV.	The Ethnic Promise Fulfilled, 1942-1965	103
V.	Unity Without Uniformity, 1965-1985	131
	Bibliographical Note	149
	Chapter Notes	151
	Appendix: Chronicle of Important Events	155
	Index	173

FOREWORD

Dr. Frank Renkiewicz, the Director of the Center for Polish Studies and Culture at the Orchard Lake Schools, is well-known to enthusiasts of Polish American history. For many years he edited *Polish American Studies,* the widely circulated and respected journal of the Polish American Historical Association. The Orchard Lake Schools are indeed fortunate to have him as a member of the faculty of St. Mary's College and director of the Center.

During the past two years Dr. Renkiewicz has compiled this social history of the Orchard Lake Schools—SS. Cyril and Methodius Seminary, St. Mary's College, and St. Mary's Preparatory—within the framework of what has been happening in Detroit, Polonia, and America since the 1870s. His history will introduce the reader to the trends and events within which individuals have acted. It will not distract the reader with a plethora of references. Those who are familiar with the history of Orchard Lake will add to it and, I hope, be inspired to carry on with research of their own. Those who learn from the work of Dr. Renkiewicz will, I believe, be strengthened in their relationship with the Orchard Lake Schools and become a significant part of their development during their second century.

Rev. Stanley Milewski
Chancellor
Orchard Lake Schools

PREFACE

Who are we, and what are we? Who and what have we been? Who and what will we be? Institutional centenaries offer unique opportunities to celebrate by rethinking the answers to those questions. The oldest participants can remember the passing of the founders while the youngest look forward to a successor generation that will be present at a second centenary when the image of the founders will have been frozen in time. Institutional memory holds a distant but vivid recollection of the adventure, driving purpose, and uncertainties of the beginning. The spirit of accomplishment and of a trust handed on by the founders is still strong among the middle-aged participants.

A centenary may be treated as a thing to be borne, gracefully and pleasureably if one is lucky, and then put behind. It also assumes a significance in itself as an occasion to remember and define the past in order to meet the future. Old symbols are invoked; departed leaders are remembered; questions are asked; values are reaffirmed; and hopes are raised. Each generation at the Polish Seminary, and more recently at the Orchard Lake Schools, has taken up the task of self-examination at quarter-century intervals—in 1910, from the perspective of a rapidly expanding immigrant community; in 1935, during a successful transition to a Polish-

American ethnic culture; and in 1960, as Polish Americans were poised to take part in a consciously pluralistic American society. Each has looked to the past in order to see the present more clearly.

The founders of the Polish Seminary in the 1880s chose consciously to implement a tradition borrowed from Poland but promptly—Father Dąbrowski especially was no prisoner of the past—adapted the tradition to American circumstances. They wrote a scenario for the preservation of Catholic Polish culture in the United States, but the script was partly a product of their immigrant history. Change was inevitable. The actors in the drama were not always its authors. Their interests and perspectives were not the same, and they used the categories of the founders in different ways. Some of them were more influential, heroic, or charismatic than others. Twice since the era of the founders, during the Grupa and Ziemba administrations, the script was edited or translated. Both times the results were similar: what happened was not entirely what the new authors wanted, but testified to the ability of cultural tradition to survive by assimilating to change.

The preparation of this manuscript also reflects the strength of tradition. The written word and documents speak their important piece, but they have limits, especially in dealing with the history of an institution that depends so much on oral tradition. I relied heavily on those who have passed on and adapted the tradition. Their willingness to speak openly and to read the manuscript critically have made the research and writing of the last two years a movable, and sometimes moving, seminar in the method and significance of history. They have suggested apt illustrations of general themes and reminders of fact as well as the perspective and judgment which flesh out the documentary skeleton. It is possible to acknowledge only a few of them here: Rev. Stanley Milewski, the Chancellor of the Orchard Lake Schools, who also guaranteed administrative support; Rev. Walter Ziemba, the immediate past Rector-President of the Schools; Rev. Leonard Chrobot, the President of St. Mary's College; Monsignor Alexander Cendrowski, whose vivid recollections embrace over two-thirds of the history of the Schools; Dr. John Gutowski, the Academic Dean of St. Mary's College; Rev. Roman Nir, who facilitated the use of the Archives of the Orchard Lake Schools; and scores of faculty members and students whose memories may not always be as long but who reminded me of the dynamism as well as the durability of tradition. They have enriched my work in different ways. The flaws and errors which survived their generous and wise assistance are mine alone.

I. *The Source*

THAT deceptively simple signature, "For God, Country, and Polonia," of the Orchard Lake Schools speaks not only to goals but to complex roots in one of Europe's oldest historic nations, Poland, and in one of the western world's newest, the United States of America.[1] The modern histories of Poland and the United States could not stand in greater contrast. Buffeted by the ambitions of neighbors and wracked by internal dissension, Poland ceased to be independent long before it disappeared from the map of Europe in 1795, victim of the last partition among Russia, Prussia, and Austria. At nearly the same moment, the United States was embarking on a political and social experiment on the western shores of the Atlantic, a prelude to world power which brought it into fateful contact with the peoples of old Poland. Except for a brief period between the World Wars of the twentieth century, when its powerful neighbors were temporarily weak, Poland has been divided or dependent on the favor of others since the Silent Sejm or Diet of 1717 surrendered control over the Republic's fortunes to Imperial Russia.

Every generation of Poles since the time of Casimir Pułaski in 1764 has risen up against its fate, and each has paid a heavy price in blood and failure: in 1794, in a last gasp of resistance to partition under Thaddeus Kościuszko; in 1830-1831, 1863-1864, and 1905 against Russian rule; in 1944, to frustrate the likely outcome of World War II; and in 1980-1981, to reverse the social and political results of that war. Defeat, however, generated the heroes, movements, issues, memories, and communal identity which created the modern nation. Patriotism everywhere depends in part on a cult of the dead, in no country more so than in Poland. Without fixed frontiers and eliminated repeatedly from the family of nations, Poland may almost be defined by its dead and by fierce loyalty to their memory.

If defeat, dependence, and resistance have been the hallmarks of Polish politics for nearly three centuries, then a sturdy Roman Catholic religious tradition has shaped—and been shaped by—Polish popular culture. Catholicism is as old as recorded history in Poland, though it never became the exclusive, dominant force it was in, say, Italy or Spain. Paganism flourished for centuries after the conversion of the Polish elite under Mieszko in 966. It was eliminated only when Catholicism absorbed and transformed the old religion in ways that are still dimly apparent in the calendar of religious folk custom. Judaism probably antedated Christianity in Poland and became a major force when Jews were expelled from most of Western Europe after the thirteenth century. The dynastic union with Lithuania in 1385 introduced a long era of contact with Europe's last pagan people. The conversion and assimilation of Lithuanians soon put Poles in direct contact with the Orthodox Christians of Byelorussia and Ukraine.

On balance, Polish Catholics preferred religious reconciliation to crusades, toleration if not tolerance, as the realistic solution to having to coexist with many other religious cultures and viewpoints. Their major experience with crusading Catholicism, the centuries-long conflict with the German Teutonic Knights, made them a principle target of religious militance. A people who also knew Moslem invaders first-hand and among whom Tartars worshipped peacefully in mosques was not likely to put much faith in the virtue of militant crusading. When Catholic predominance was threatened during the Protestant Reformation in the sixteenth and early seventeenth centuries, Poles reacted characteristically. Repression of dissenters was the exception rather than the rule and, as in the expulsion of the anti-Trinitarian Arians in 1658, was undertaken for political more than for religious reasons.

Polish Catholics had neither the will nor the power to impose their views consistently upon others. Instead, they responded to the Reformation with an "extreme inward piety" which set them off from other Poles and external enemies. The Polish Counter-Reformation emphasized pilgrimage and the path of Calvary, unworldliness in religious orders and disdain for material possessions, public and communal acts of penance, and the veneration of saints who stood for those values. Lay confraternities flourished to recite the rosary, to pray at length, and to process. Above all, Polish Catholics met the challenge of Jews, Protestants, and Orthodox through veneration of the Virgin Mary. There were over a thousand shrines to Mary in Poland in the seventeenth century. The Pauline Monastery of Jasna Góra (the Bright Mountain) at Częstochowa was only the most famous of them. The ceremonial coronation of Our Lady at Częstochowa as "Queen of Poland" in 1717, the year in which the Polish government formally subordinated itself to Russia, demonstrated the will of the Church to hold its own among the masses against all challengers. It was also, many have added, a reaffirmation of the native "Old Polish" tradition against the centralizing, Latinizing, Romanizing demands of the Catholic Reformation built on the Council of Trent.

When Austria, Prussia, and Russia finally disposed of the Polish state in 1795, each power took care to bring the institutional Church to heel. Bishoprics were allowed to lie vacant or were filled with pliable administrators. Privileges were curtailed, and Church affairs were treated as matters of utmost political expediency. The policy took its most virulent form in the Russian empire. After the insurrection of 1830-1831, half the Roman Catholic convents of the Russian partition were closed, and payment of the salaries of the clergy was assumed by the state. All sermons, pronouncements, and religious publications had to be approved by the Tsarist censorship and all seminaries inspected by the Tsarist police.

More punitive measures were adopted in the aftermath of the January, 1863 rising. Most Catholic religious communities in Russian Poland were dissolved, and all estates of the Church and of lay patrons of Catholic benefices were confiscated. The Ministry of the Interior and lay, police-approved delegates assumed direction of internal church affairs. Unauthorized correspondence with Rome was punishable by summary deportation. In 1870, the introduction of a Russian-language liturgy provoked open conflict in the diocese of Wilno. In its zeal to curb all signs of Polish national consciousness the Russian government stopped just short of wholesale closure of Roman Catholic churches.

The Kingdom of Prussia and the new German Empire, which Prussia dominated after 1871, pursued similar policies more gradually and within the framework of law, but ultimately with the same goal as Russia. The Kulturkampf of the 1870s, a largely Prussian phenomenon, subjected the Catholic Church to state control, dissolved most religious orders and congregations, and interrupted communications between the Church in Germany and the Vatican. As the largest Catholic minority in Prussia, Poles felt the force of those and a score of other repressive measures more than most. Even such a cooperative churchman as Mieczysław Ledochowski, the Archbishop of Poznań-Gniezno, chose imprisonment in 1874-1876 rather than submit to the demand of the Prussian government that the religious instruction of young Polish children be conducted in German. The formal end of the Kulturkampf after 1883 was followed by a spate of administrative acts and laws to colonize Germans on Polish-owned estates and to eliminate the Polish language from public use.

Germanization failed while provoking the very national consciousness it sought to repress. Poles mounted a successful campaign of their own to hold and expand their land holdings. The language issue became the touchstone of cultural resistance. A school strike in Września, near Poznań, protested the introduction of German into religious education in 1901; and school strikes in 1906-1907 touched nearly half the schools of the province of Poznań. Organizations, newspapers, and political actions multiplied to protest and circumvent the attack on Polish culture.

The Vatican, motivated by a conservative social philosophy and a desire to preserve a measure of authority over local churches, did little to support national aspirations or social change in Poland during the partition period. The Polish episcopate, when it was allowed to function normally, failed with few exceptions to do more than the popes. It fell to the lower clergy, directly in touch with the masses, to associate the Church with the goals and deepest values of Polish society in the last half of the nineteenth century. Often involved in radical political and social movements themselves, priests and religious somehow remained mostly loyal to their superiors as they earned what now seems a traditional leadership role among ordinary Poles.

The founding fathers of Polish-American Catholicism were confronted by a social as well as cultural awakening in both their old country and their new home. The immigrants they led were drawn mostly from the Polish peasantry, a loose social term embracing everyone from impoverished farm workers to prosperous landholders. Whatever their economic rank, they had been obliged to perform service for local landlords as the price of residence, the use of farm land, and access to communal properties such as meadows, forests, and lakes. Their values were reflected not only in their Catholicism, but also in an abiding faith in an authoritarian family structure and real estate as sources of emotional and economic security.

When the occupying powers took control in the late eighteenth century, the unpopular labor service requirements, especially in Russia, grew more onerous. Then, in the nineteenth century, the same powers liberated peasants from obligations to serve on estates and to live in their home districts. Native Polish leaders, deeply involved as *szlachta* or nobility in the landholding system, were unable to agree on an adequate and timely response to peasant aspirations for bread and freedom. Their failure to solve the social question in the country weighed heavily in the defeat of repeated national insurrections against foreign rule from 1794 to 1864. Shrewd peasants saw no point in fighting for a Poland they did not own, and the partition governments took temporary advantage of that calculus of interest to build loyalty to themselves.

Serfdom died for other reasons, of course, chiefly the need to modernize and rationalize creaking societies and economies. Prussia, where the process began in 1808, learned from its defeat by Napoleon that a modern state could not survive on an exploited, immobile, and uneducated rural underclass. It simply was not efficient. Impatient with the early results, the government accelerated the reform toward mid-century and completed it in the 1850s. Emancipation came more suddenly in the other partitions: in Austrian Galicia to punish patriot landlords in 1846-48; and in Russian Poland, in 1864, by a czarist government eager to outbid Polish nationalists, many of them noble landlords, for the loyalty of peasants. Eventually, the great landlords reconciled themselves to emancipation as they witnessed the consequences of a reformed labor system. A competitive and mobile labor force reduced a major cost of agriculture. The elimination of small holdings, because their tenants could not afford to buy out of the old system and into the new, opened new prospects for large-scale farming. The conversion of communal lands into private property also increased the size of large holdings and the likelihood that the new wage-labor work force would find employment. Estates and big farms survived as more profitable, commercial, agricultural enterprises.

Emancipation did not solve the social question in the Polish countryside at all. Peasants soon discovered that personal freedom and the end of serfdom did not normally confer the advantages of land ownership or force employers to compete for their labor. Most simply lost the elemental support they had under the old system, became "free" farm laborers, or, as in central Galicia, lived precariously on small, marginal plots of land. An unforeseen but crushing rise in population in many parts of Galicia and Russian Poland after 1870 threatened to deprive many of even the little they had won.

A significant minority of peasants, notably in Prussia, acquired sufficient land to turn a profit. Guided at first by intelligent and enlightened landlords and later on their own, many peasants turned to a variety of self-help organizations —consumer cooperatives, savings and loan banks, associations for joint purchase of machinery or breeding stock, schools, and populist political parties. The Polish village, in which even private family affairs were matters of general concern, provided a framework for spontaneous social action. Under the slogan "organic work" the Polish leadership developed an apolitical program for the social progress of all classes through economic self-help. "We want to extend work and learning in society," proclaimed one of their number in the aftermath of the failure of the insurrection of 1863, "to discover new resources, to utilize existing ones, and to concern ourselves with our own problems and not those of others."[2] His was also a virtual credo for the first immigrant generation in America.

The alternative to limited upward mobility on native soil was migration for work within the Polish countryside, to the growing cities of Poland, westward to the industrial German Rhineland (and to Belgium and France after 1919), eastward to central Russia and Siberia, and, ultimately, overseas to the semi-tropical forests of Brazil and to the farms and factories of the United States. Poles from Prussia (Kaszubia and Poznań mainly) led the move to America from the 1850s to the 1880s, at first to the new farmlands and then to the cities of the Midwest. Migration from Galicia and Russian Poland became dominant in the 1890s, cresting in the decade before the First World War. It resumed after the War, ending only with restrictive American immigration laws in 1921 and 1924. Altogether, some 3.1 million ethnic Poles emigrated to all parts of the world. Perhaps as many left and returned home, and several times that number were affected through personal ties to emigrants. Between 1.8 and 2.2 million Poles may have come to the United States, all but a fraction of them during 1855-1930. Many moved back and forth across the Atlantic in response to the economic cycle, but the great majority (as many as 1.5 million) settled permanently in the United States to create an immigrant community whose descendants numbered over eight million in the 1980s.

II. *The Polish Seminary*

POLISH America was founded in the economic modernization of east-central Europe. It was shaped by a complex Catholic tradition, economic scarcity in the countryside, and political statelessness. The outlines of the social and institutional structure of Polonia, as it was called, were apparent in the earliest settlements like Panna Maria, Texas, in 1854, and in other rural colonies like Polonia, Wisconsin, and Parisville, Michigan, which dotted the Midwest soon afterward. If Polonia had a core institution, it was probably the church parish, for the most part a reworking of the old village within an urban, industrializing economy. At least 900 churches arose to serve immigrants and their children. Normally, in the early years, they were founded by lay societies which gathered money, purchased land for a building, and often recruited a priest-pastor in cooperation with the local bishop. Sometimes communities were born with strong clerical leadership. Panna Maria, where the Conventual Franciscan priest, Rev. Leopold Moczygemba, led a core of settlers from the Opole region of Silesia, was a good example. Usually, however, lay leadership predominated at the beginning. But after some hesitations, nearly every successful community found a priest who built the stable center around which it flourished. The new churches themselves generated a host of organizations to meet their material and spiritual needs by involving each class of members in their communal life.

What happened was that Poles adapted to their new circumstances by fitting traditional forms and values into borrowed institutions. The territorial parish in Poland became the national parish in America, and there was talk from the 1870s to about 1900 of a Polish Catholic ecclesiastical jurisdiction transcending diocesan boundaries in the United States. The American bishops would not hear of a Polish bishop at first—the clumsy response of some of them to ethnic aspirations spurred schismatic Independent Catholic church movements—but they were compelled, finally, to tolerate an informal Polish sub-community within the American Church. Meanwhile, thousands of voluntary associations sprouted to satisfy every impulse to social action from singing to military training. Separate from but in a symbiotic relationship with the church, they often adopted benefit programs to protect members' families from the uncertainties of death or sickness. Bound together in national organizations like the Polish National Alliance and the Polish Roman Catholic Union, these mutual aid societies insured their members against the loss of life, physical health, and cultural values.

Joseph Dąbrowski, one of the chief architects of Polish America, led a life which is the stuff of historical generalizations and legends. Born into a family of the lesser landed nobility in the village of Żółtańce in the Russian partition in 1842, he completed his primary and secondary education in nearby Lublin. In 1862, he entered the Szkoła Główna or "Main School," as the restored University of Warsaw was then known, where he seemed headed toward a career as an engineer. Everything predisposed him to be swept up in the January Insurrection of 1863: no first-hand knowledge of the failure of the previous uprising in 1830; a background in the educated lower-middle class which supplied most of the recruits for Polish national movements throughout the century; and the heady atmosphere of student life in Warsaw, where a brief relaxation of Russian rule in the early 1860s encouraged dreams of independence.

The utter defeat of the January Insurrection, the failure of peasants to rally to the Polish cause, and the sheer power of Russia left a deep mark on Dąbrowski's generation. National leaders turned decisively to the philosophy of "organic work." Rooted in an old view that Poland's problems were the result of internal weakness, organic work renounced the use of armed struggle for independence as useless and counter-productive in the foreseeable future. Instead, as advocates of political and social realism, the post-1863 leadership invested its energies in the long-term improvement of society through education and economic development. A temperance movement, in which priests were often prominent, sought to reform the drinking habits of country folk to prepare them for the demands of modern politics, agricultural efficiency, or the routine of urban factories. The approach of the realists often amounted to support for unbridled industrial capitalism and for landowners who would convert serfs into "free" and efficient but dependent tenants and workers. The realists willingly risked the consequences and let others (Catholic activists and socialists) worry about remedies. The American Dąbrowski shared something of their basic philosophy. He was never known as a sentimental dreamer. Disillusion with the consequences of the romantic spirit of 1863-65 may explain the strength of an outburst in later life: "All manner of boasting, empty publicity, in fact all vain display is unspeakably hateful to me. I abhor it because it spells perdition."[1]

Forced to leave Poland for his part in the January Insurrection, Dąbrowski went first to Dresden, then to Switzerland for two years, and finally to Rome where he joined the charter class of the Polish Papal College in 1866 to prepare for the priesthood. The Rector of the College, Father Peter Semenenko, had collaborated with two other soldier-scholars, Bogdan Janski and Jerome Kajsiewicz, in founding the Congregation of the Resurrection in 1836. The Resurrectionists were themselves a product of disillusion with romantic revolution and of a Catholic revival after the failure of the November Insurrection. Father Semenenko dedicated himself to eradicating, as blasphemous secularism, the excesses of Polish Romantic Messianism, the view that Poland, as the suffering Christ among nations, would play a leading role in the emancipation of mankind from worldly oppression. Turning his back on the romanticism of his youth, Semenenko joined the struggle against the nineteenth-century Roman Catholic trinity of vices—socialism, modernism, and materialism—through "the organization of secular priests leading the religious life" and "religious having the calling of secular priests." Such priests, he believed, would hold back the tide of secular materialism by building a network of community-parishes saturated with service organizations of all kinds. Unable to resist their socially attractive power and the religious message which created them, Semenenko reasoned, the newly urbanizing Polish masses would be tied firmly to their old Church.

Joseph Dąbrowski absorbed Semenenko's message as did contemporaries like Father Vincent Barzyński, another refugee of the January Uprising, who, shortly after taking his final vows as a Resurrectionist in Rome in September, 1866, embarked on a major career as a pastor in Texas and Chicago. Soon after his ordination in August, 1869, Dąbrowski took the advice of Father Leopold Moczygemba, the founder of Panna Maria in 1854, and accepted an invitation from the Bishop of Green Bay to work among the Polish immigrants of Wisconsin. Arriving in New York on the last day of 1869, and in Milwaukee early in the new year, Dąbrowski was assigned to the remote, rural settlement of Poland Corner in the central part of the state. A few months later he reported from there to his former rector in Rome: "Our Polish people are living without the Mass, confession, Sunday sermons, and adequate education. Some have settled in the large cities and, because of the lack of priests and the preaching of the Word of God, do not attend church services. Without any religious formation, they will certainly be lost to the Church."[2] The young priest proposed to attack the problem by establishing a seminary to prepare priests for Polish parish work in America, an idea which failed to generate a positive response from his Resurrectionist mentor. The remainder of the young priest's life, nevertheless, amounted to a campaign to fill the void in the religious formation of the new immigrants.

The Resurrectionist program and the clear absence of priests for immigrants lend credibility to Dąbrowski's later claim that Polish bishops, including Archbishop Mieczysław Ledochowski, pressed by requests for help from America, proposed a seminary in America to fill the need. Contemporary records, however, show only more limited plans. The Polish Roman Catholic Union of America (PRCUA), founded in 1873 "to uphold the Catholic Faith and our national heritage through the promotion of Catholic learning and instruction," wanted to establish a secondary school which might also function as a minor seminary.[3] During Rev. Leopold Moczygemba's tenure as president of the PRCUA in 1875-1878, the Union decided to locate the school in Nebraska, where it proposed to build a colony on land purchased from the Burlington-Missouri Railroad. Presumably, the Resurrectionists were to implement and administer the project through Father Moczygemba.

During a long visit to Rome, beginning in July, 1878, Moczygemba altered the school plan, in effect combining the seminary and secondary school projects of the previous years. He prepared a petition to the new Pope, Leo XIII, outlining the need for Polish priests in America to serve an immigration estimated at 200,000 souls. By way of remedy he proposed a college and seminary "for young men of this nationality who wished to dedicate themselves to the religious life" and asked for "permission to designate for this purpose all of the funds that are presently in his possession, and all other funds which he will be able to receive in the future." Leo XIII approved the petition on January 14, 1879, with this inscription: *"Annuimus in omnibus juxta petita. Leo P.P. XIII."* ("We agree to everything according to your petition. Pope Leo XIII.")[4]

Father Moczygemba stayed on in Rome for another year while he formally joined the Resurrectionist Congregation. Returning to Chicago in April, 1880, he found the situation changed. The PRCUA was floundering. The colonization project in Nebraska had fallen far short of the hopes for it. Polish immigration, by shifting strongly to the cities in the economic recovery after the depression of the 1870s, had undermined a major premise of the project. Moreover, a new grouping of immigrant organizations led by lay nationalists was about to come into existence as the Polish National Alliance (PNA). Opposed to the pretensions of the Resurrectionists to dominate the immigrants through the PRCUA, the leaders of the Alliance soon entered into a bitter struggle with the clericalist Union for influence in Polonia. Moczygemba went ahead, nevertheless, purchasing some 350 acres in Nebraska as a school site for $1,900 in June, 1880. A few weeks later he wrote Father Semenenko, his new superior in Rome: "The plan or idea of the Polish college will work if we only get started, because intelligent Poles and certain bishops feel the need of such an institution and desire its realization."[5]

Father Dąbrowski, meanwhile, had harnassed his formidable sense of purpose to pastoral and educational work in Wisconsin. True to his grass-roots philosophy of social improvement, he had quickly moved his church from Poland Corner, a rowdy neighborhood of taverns, a mile and a half away to the peaceful precincts of Polonia where his advocacy of temperance and hard work stood a better chance of being heard. In 1874, he had brought the first Felician sisters from Poland to staff the parochial school he was building on the American public model. Both he and his Resurrectionist colleagues had been in touch with the sisters since the late 1860s. As their American director, Dąbrowski guided the Felicians spirtually and taught them the "elements of pedagogy." Sometimes his optimism had the best of him. Prior to their arrival, he advised the sisters, mistakenly, that they "would learn English in a short time, because the English language is very easy, only the orthography is very curious, but that too can be learned easily."[6] He was also clear, and more realistic, about his educational goals: "In our curriculum we must adhere to that of the public schools, which follow the plan I outlined above, and under no circumstances can we allow ourselves to take second place to the Protestants in this area, who value education very highly."⁷

Without sacrificing either Polish culture or Catholicism, Father Dąbrowski promptly set about the task of not allowing "ourselves to take second place to the Protestants," an effort which eventually won him the reputation as the founder of the Polish-American school system. Young women were recruited to the Felicians as aspirants or postulants, giving the new province a decidedly American character. The practical emphasis of their education in secular subjects, often taught by Dąbrowski himself, and their preparation to teach also set them off from their European sisters. Since there were no materials for the schools they were about to serve, Dąbrowski, in collaboration with the sisters, wrote and printed in the church's printshop at least three pioneering Polish-American textbooks (a Polish reader and geography and arithmetic texts) during their Wisconsin years. These were the first of 45 Polish-American textbooks which they produced, printed, and distributed between 1877 and 1904. For a while, also, these Polish partners in the Wisconsin wilderness hoped to embrace Native Americans in their mission. Dąbrowski preached to the Chippewa, Winnebago, and Menominee, baptized several hundred into his church, and taught his new flock the ways of Euro-American agriculture. His Polish-Chippewa dictionary was designed to facilitate the mission; and, for a brief while, until they reverted to their previous lives, Native Americans also joined the Felician community.

Themselves, like Dąbrowski and many others, the victims of repression in Russian Poland in 1864, the Felicians had survived as a community only by moving their headquarters from Warsaw to Cracow in the Austrian partition in the following year. Though perceived as "dangerous revolutionaries" by the Russian authorities, they were the very soul of "organic work," ministering to the poor and the orphans of industrial society. In America they did that and under Dąbrowski's watchful eye, added education to their mission. Within a few years, they staffed six schools outside Polonia, opened an orphanage in LaSalle, Illinois, and were tapping the wellsprings of religious devotion and professional ambition among the daughters of immigrants who applied for membership.

Rural Wisconsin was not, any more than rural Nebraska, an ideal place to build an organization for reaching large numbers of new immigrants to the city. By the fall of 1879, when the Felicians began to teach at St. Albertus in Detroit, the superior of the congregation in America was certain that the city would be important to their future. On November 21, 1879, she asked permission of the Superior General in Europe to move the headquarters to a centrally located city where the sisters would enjoy more support from priests and other religious. Father Dąbrowski's health was another factor in leaving the physically demanding life in rural Wisconsin. Bishop Borgess of Detroit was receptive to their plans; and in 1880, they began construction of a motherhouse on St. Aubin Street, across from St. Albertus. The new motherhouse opened in October, 1882, and included a convent and a teacher training school. The Seminary of the Felician Sisters, an institution at about the level of a junior high school, which Dąbrowski founded, directed, and served as a teacher, evolved into a normal school. St. Albertus' School served as their laboratory school. Urged on by Dąbrowski, its graduates won diocesan and state certification, making the Felicians by far the largest group of Polish-American professionals in Detroit by the turn of the century. Dąbrowski also made the motherhouse his home and sometime during the next eighteen months took up the work of building a Polish seminary in America.

The Detroit community which Father Dąbrowski encountered in 1882 was like many other Polonias scattered across the American Midwest. It had taken root in the late 1850s and the 1860s with immigrants from Prussia, mainly Kashubs from the region south and west of Danzig who were soon followed by Poznanians. They had found their first homes and Catholic churches on the city's east side among Germans, whose language was familiar to them. The German neighborhood was developing eastward along Gratiot Avenue toward Mt. Elliot, then the city's eastern boundary.

Poles established their historic path of settlement by moving north along streets like St. Aubin where in 1872, at the intersection with Canfield, they built their first church, St. Albertus. By the early 1880s there were 1,200 families in the parish and perhaps as many as 15,000 Poles in a city which numbered nearly 125,000. A second major westward corridor of settlement had opened up by then along Michigan Avenue from about 20th Street to 25th and beyond the city's border into Springwells.

The earliest immigrants were often skilled tradesmen who laid the foundations for the ethnic community's business middle class. Detroit's factories and foundries—the city was the center of stove-making in the U.S.—offered work to the masses, however. Galician Poles, who became numerous after 1880, were more likely to find unskilled work: if men, in railway car shops and construction or in excavation; if women, as domestics, washerwomen or cigar makers. Both men and women were employed as farm hands for the Ferry Seed Company. Voluntary associations, often with a mutual aid feature in case of sickness or death, accommodated every conceivable interest—paramilitary and gymnastic, dramatic and singing, charitable and devotional, educational and literary. Institutional completeness eventually made it unnecessary to deal with outsiders, who in any case were usually recent immigrants from other European countries.

Polonia's values were shaped by an overwhelming sense of material scarcity—not the uncertainly that once had come from waiting for the next harvest in peasant Poland, but the kind created by the vagaries of the business cycle in industrial America. Behavior that outsiders often wondered at flowed from having to depend on a small and unpredictable surplus of income. The first Polish-Americans responded to their predicament in a variety of ways. Early immigrants were notable for their indifference to the quality of the goods they consumed and the social status of their work. Savings and income were more important than style. Family members earned and pooled income in a variety of ways—young children through simple tasks such as gathering firewood, mothers by gardening and housework, older children by dropping out of school and entering service or factory work. Some commentators have called such immigrant and later ethnic behavior thrift, a work ethic or love of family, when in fact it represented a practical and frequently successful readjustment to the urban, industrial world.

Scarcity also induced a passionate search for security through ownership of a small home on a narrow city lot. The cost of a lot in Detroit's Polish colony rose from about $300 in 1883 to about $1,250 in 1900. Terms were easy, however: usually twenty-five dollars down, seven percent interest, and five dollar monthly payments. The closeness of Polish neighborhoods and the reluctance of outsiders to buy into them held the values of real estate below comparable properties elsewhere. During the 1880s and 1890s, the long rows of single and two-family homes in the St. Albertus area expanded north to Grand Boulevard and east to McDougall Street. The streetcar lines which were laid down from 1892 confirmed the pattern of Detroit's growth, determining the location of factories and the movement of population along the major arteries which radiated from the city's center. As Poles moved north or west into previously undeveloped country, the areas they had taken from Germans were occupied by a medley of peoples—southern American Blacks, Italians, east European Jews—who gave Hastings Street and Gratiot Avenue a cosmopolitan, Euro-American atmosphere. The classic pattern of ethnic succession also appeared early within the community itself as Russian Poles replaced Prussian Poles, who headed north in the 1890s.

What was the purpose of education in this fledgling Polonia? Americans have usually linked formal education to social or economic mobility, sometimes to personal growth. Polish immigrants and their children seldom connected education with a change in social status or economic class. The leadership in Polonia often criticized the parochial school system for that failure and for the apparently slow economic progress of American Poles. Polish immigrants, their children and many of their grandchildren, however, were not preoccupied with upward social or class mobility (an elusive goal anyway for most immigrants in America) but rather with more income for a better life within their social or class rank. Schooling served other purposes. It supported religious values and family, goals reflected in the habit of children (boys especially) dropping out after First Communion in order to meet the demands of parents that they contribute to family income. It supported authority everywhere in church, family, and society through the tough discipline imposed by the sisters. By doing little to encourage children to pursue exceptional material goods for themselves, Polish-American schools also reinforced an immigrant critique of the role of the "almighty dollar" in American culture.

Higher education for Polish-Americans was founded upon similar values. Whatever occasional intellectual hopes they kindled, college and university appealed to Polonia mainly to educate priests to guide a rapidly growing population. American bishops would have preferred to draw upon their own seminaries for priests, but that was not practical in most large Polish centers until the 1920s. Since secular priests from Poland were uncertain quantities at best, the bishops turned to religious communities like Conventual Franciscans, Jesuits and Resurrectionists, and to seminaries in Rome and Louvain for better priests. Eventually, Polish-American provinces of religious communities established seminaries of their own. None of these was more than a partial or short-term solution, however; and in the early 1880s, the need was immediate and overwhelming. Many American bishops felt compelled to accept some other institution to form priests who spoke Polish and were sensitive to Polish culture.

Finally, enough Polish-American Catholics were as eager to establish a seminary of their own as they had been to found a separate ecclesiastical jurisdiction, making it likely they would contribute money and recruits. Dąbrowski caught their mood by appealing to the roots of their culture and the recent immigration experience. Though eager to match the Anglo-American achievement, he was unable and unwilling to sacrifice Polonia's cultural heritage. "Our well understood interest in the matter of our religion and nationality," he wrote to the Polish priests of America, "demands that Poles hold together not relinquishing their nationality. Religion teaches us to love God above all else and to love everything else in God. Therefore, we are to love our nationality honestly and in God. Religion does not exclude love of country and love of nationality. Rather it ennobles it. The Church forbids caprices and slavish worship of nationality. On the other hand, our nation is deeply Catholic, and as long as Poles will be Poles, that fact will be a great mainstay of our religion. In this way our religion and nationality support each other."[8]

To those who argued that young Polish-Americans should be educated immediately in American institutions, Dąbrowski countered realistically that "A young man upon leaving elementary school does not know the [Polish] language sufficiently and if he remains in an English seminary for a long period of time, he will forget everything and will be a Pole who does not know Polish and upon becoming a priest will do well for the Germans and the English but not for the Poles." Dąbrowski was immensely practical about the status of Poles in America. "Let us not delude ourselves," he told their priests, "that we have achieved a high status in this country. Oratorical agitation and involvement in political machinations, into which at times others pull us for their own benefit, is not the proper status for our nation. Such a thing can be appropriate in certain times and sometimes exclusively for some people, but value for a nation resides in education and virtue—a people with understanding and virtue based on religion. We shall arrive at that stage only through our various institutions, which will cultivate and sustain religion, education, as well as nationality based on religion and organized in such a way that in a given situation it would both satisfy our needs and make us secure for the future. Having attained our proper status [on our own], we might remain there and not look to the favors of others to do something for us."[9] The argument for organic work and Catholic survival could not have been stated more succinctly.

Need and preference created the Polish Seminary in America. The catalyst in the process was the chaplain-director of the Felicians. Sometime before 1884, Father Moczygemba placed the Seminary project into Father Dąbrowski's hands and agreed to transfer the site and assets of the proposed school from Nebraska to Detroit. In February, 1884, Dąbrowski began negotiations with his bishop, Casper Borgess, to open a "college" to prepare young Poles for the priesthood. His plans for an "ecclesiastical seminary" also included a "necessary few preparatory classes," the forerunner of the classics department and preparatory high school.[10] Bishop Borgess, perhaps prepared by his German birth and American training and by similar aspirations among German Americans to see the point of it all, authorized Dąbrowski on March 14, 1884, "to solicit aid for this important undertaking in our diocese, and beg to recommend you to the kind consideration of the Right Reverend Bishops of other Dioceses who may share in the benefit of the institution."[11] As a major seminary or theologate under the jurisdiction of the Bishop of Detroit, it was meant to serve the needs of dioceses throughout America.

Dąbrowski moved quickly in April to purchase land, just over two acres, for the Seminary on St. Aubin Avenue between Forest and Garfield streets. The site, one block north of the Felician Motherhouse and St. Albertus church, was on the city's edge, and still reminded visitors of boggy farmlands "where you could shoot a duck in the spring and later catch crabs and frogs."[12] Dąbrowski borrowed $5,000 to cover the purchase price until the sale of the Nebraska lands went through in August. Father Moczygemba contributed about $8,000 from that sale and from earlier collections to buy the land and initiate building. Ground was broken on May 19, 1885, and the cornerstone was laid during an impressive ceremony on July 22, 1885, when the Seminary was dedicated to SS. Cyril and Methodius.

The Apostles to the Slavs had been objects of increasing interest in recent years. The feast of SS. Cyril and Methodius had been incorporated into the universal Church calendar in 1880, and millennial celebrations of their achievement occurred widely in 1885. The choice of the patronal name reflected that interest as well as a hope that the new school would appeal to other Slavic immigrant groups in America. For reasons having more to do with contemporary popular piety, the new seminary was also erected in the name of the Immaculate Conception of Mary. Though called St. Mary's or SS. Cyril and Methodius Seminary, the new school was usually known as the Polish Seminary, a name that was occasionally stretched into Polish Academy and even the Polish University. It was only during the time of the First World War that the high school began routinely to call itself St. Mary's. When the same name was applied to the college level program in the early 1920s, the seminary proper began consistently to use SS. Cyril and Methodius to identify itself. Whatever the internal designations, the title "Polish Seminary" clung to the three schools in the minds of most people for the better part of their first century.

The opening of the Seminary building for classes, scheduled for the fall, had to be delayed until December, 1886, and then only in a scaled-down version and with the help of the first seminarians in finishing the final stages of construction. The short but sharp depression of 1884-1886 also hampered fund-raising just as Detroit Polonia was being asked to finance two other large projects: to the west, where the new St. Casimir's parish was trying to pay the debt on a church and school erected in 1883; and at St. Albertus itself, where parishioners committed themselves in March, 1884, to a magnificent new church under the direction of the flamboyant and charismatic Father Dominik Kolasiński. Known as the "largest Polish Church in America," the new St. Albertus was blessed one week before the Seminary cornerstone was dedicated.

Father Kolasiński was physically and temperamentally the antithesis of Father Dąbrowski, whom one reporter described in 1886 as "laying no claim to personal attractions. He . . . wears a black fur cap pulled down on the left side of his head. His Roman collar is the only mark to distinguish that he is a priest. He has a full dark-complexioned face and expressionless black eyes."[13] Years later, in 1900, Dąbrowski impressed an admiring visitor in much the same way, as having the "appearance of a laborer, rough, tanned, suggesting toughness and strength . . . ." [14] No match for Kolasiński in popular appeal, Dąbrowski succeeded the colorful pastor at St. Albertus following his suspension by Bishop Borgess for financial and other irregularities in November, 1885. Dąbrowski withdrew in March, 1887, from direct involvement in this frequently sensational controversy about style and power in Polonia's churches, but he was dogged by its consequences for a decade. His statement on the occasion of the laying of the Seminary cornerstone constituted a realistic philosphy of what and in what order he thought Polonia should be about. It was also in part a response to Kolasiński's supporters: "I have in view the education of the Polish candidates for the priesthood and the education of others, so that they may be on a par with other young men in this country. Heretofore we have been obliged to procure Polish priests from Europe, but they cannot speak English and cannot do what a native American might. We Poles have the right to enjoy complete liberty in this country, but liberty cannot be enjoyed fully by uneducated people. The better a people is educated, the better they enjoy liberty and the better citizens they become of America." He concluded with a thinly veiled reference to his nemesis: "I deem the erection of this seminary more necessary than the building of expensive churches. Intelligence only makes men free."[15]

The academic framework within which Dąbrowski hoped to promote the "intelligence" to do "what a native American might" took shape in the next few years. It had two major characteristics: the existence of a classical or preparatory department in conjunction with a theological seminary; and the use of Polish, English and Latin in instruction, anticipating a century of social and cultural history. The seminary proper had two sections: a two-year sequence called philosophy and a final three-year theology program. The courses were the ones prescribed by the Church for the preparation of priests and others that were part of a normal college curriculum. Theology was taught in Latin; the humanities mostly in Polish; geography, mathematics, the sciences, and English, of course, in English. The first ordinations from the theologate took place in 1890.

Spiritual formation was initially in the hands of Father Dąbrowski. Father Buhaczkowski, the second rector, probably appointed the first official spiritual director and, in 1909, divided the office in two, one each for theology and philosophy. In the early years Dąbrowski himself preached on Sundays, occasionally delegating confessions and leadership in prayer life to Fathers Michael Barabasz or Leon Jarecki. As one might expect in a Catholic seminary, the liturgy of the mass dominated the schedule. Forty-Hours in October and the Feasts of St. Stanislaus Kostka in November and of St. Joseph in March were the other major devotional events. Ceremonies of investiture, "the donning of the black cassock," and tonsure, "the making of a cleric," were the initial public ceremonies in a seminarian's progress to ordination. The Jesuit Father Francis Szulak, active in mission work throughout Middle West Polonia in the late nineteenth century, conducted the early annual retreats—a contribution recognized by his nomination as the Seminary's first honorary alumnus in 1899. The only recorded spiritual organization in the Seminary's immigrant era was the Society of the Sacred Heart, established in 1903 to promote devotion to the Sacred Heart, encourage moral conduct through good example, and maintain the chapels.

As early as 1888, the Polish Seminary embraced two schools. Though the theology department stirred greater public interest and motivated the building of the Seminary, the classics course, later known as the high school and the preparatory, quickly and quietly grew larger. The reason was practical. As Father Dąbrowski put it to the American bishops in 1884: "The course of study and the discipline will be similar to those in the other ecclesiastical institutions in this country. But as we have to begin with young men who have only received an elementary education, the preparatory course will have to be introduced at least for a time."[16] The Polish Seminary was not and never became the type of segregated institution for the preparation of priests envisioned by the Council of Trent and created by many American archdioceses in the twentieth century. Like most American seminaries of the late nineteenth century it depended on young students for survival.

The five-year classics program was modeled on the European gymnasium, the last year equivalent to the first in an American college. Each grade studied religion, Polish, Latin, English, and mathematics; the first two also took courses in geography, penmanship, zoology, and botany; the last three, Greek, history, physics, and chemistry. French and German were also offered. From 1902 to 1921, a special class was also offered to prepare deficient or very young students for classics. Textbooks were mostly those used in contemporary Galicia where German examples and methods provided the major inspiration.

Polish and English were the languages of instruction, no small issue in an immigrant Polish environment. As one alumnus recalled long afterward, there was "quite a difference in character and disposition between the American-born boys and those who came from Europe."[17] Both groups "had a bewildering mixture of Polish and English in their vocabularies," but socio-linguistic distinctions based on origin in America or Poland or in some part of Poland (Poznań, Galicia or Warsaw, for example) soon became an important part of student society.

During the 1890s, the Seminary also attracted many students from populations that had been in historic relation with European Poland. At commencement in 1894, students spoke in nine languages: Latin, Greek, Polish, Ukrainian, Russian, French, German, Lithuanian, and English. Lithuanians, who were becoming more conscious of their national and linguistic identity in the late nineteenth century, were particularly important. Their language was introduced into the classics curriculum in 1895; Lithuanian students formed a separate section of the "Polish" Literary Society under the patronage of St. Casimir, their national saint; and Lithuanian priests were a factor in the first alumni association in 1899. Father Buhaczkowski, the second rector and practically co-founder of the Seminary, was himself born in Lithuania. Lithuanian student enrollment reached a peak of about 25 shortly after the move to Orchard Lake in 1909. Though they occasionally felt slighted by their Polish colleagues, the Lithuanian students matured into important pastors, editors, and cultural leaders of their ethnic community. Their number dwindled after World War I, and their club—it had become chapter one of the Alliance of Lithuanian Roman Catholic Students of America—disappeared from campus.

Clearly the Seminary taught more than subject matter. It formed priests and ethnic Americans. The introduction of night classes for immigrants in 1896 gave it occasion for declaring a philosophy of language and culture which had grown naturally out of Father Dąbrowski's experience in rural Wisconsin and formed a credo for the future: "Everyone knows that the English language is indispensable to us in America, not only in mutual intercourse, business, industry, but also in public life . . . ignorance of it bars for many the way to public offices to which we have equal right with other nationalities. We must learn English! . . . let us love our own tongue and everything ours is good and dear to our heart and memory, but let him, who will neglect the English language in the English environment, be sure that he will often meet with neglect from Englishmen . . . ."[18]

Secondary education for young immigrants had been the germ of the Seminary project in the early 1870s, and it supported the success of the outcome here as it did in many other early Catholic American seminaries. The classics department supplied both needed income and recruits to the higher school. It was consistently three-quarters or more of the general enrollment as the whole institution grew from six students at its opening to 154 in 1900 and 326 in 1909. However, many classics students boarded at home, and most did not go on to theological studies. By 1899, Father Dąbrowski indirectly acknowledged that most of his young charges were interested in other callings: "the purpose of the Polish Seminary is the education of Polish youth in a religious, moral and national spirit, and at the same time, by the means of classical training, modern languages, the natural sciences and the like in the high school curriculum to prepare the youth for future professions: namely, sacred theology taught at the institution after the completion of a two-year philosophical course, or lay professions: law, medicine, technical studies, and the like."[19]

The three divisions of the Seminary were indispensable to each other. Curricula meshed, and faculties overlapped; but students did not always enjoy the unity of a common administration. The rebellious theologians of 1903 believed "that the younger students were altogether too familiar and did not show a proper respect for those who by their years of study were entitled to wear the cassock." They demanded "the separation of the theologians from the classics" and "a rule to make the freshmen treat their elders with proper respect."[20] The wish for a stricter seminary atmosphere was granted eventually, and the schools adopted a policy of strict social separation between classics and philosophy-theology. They also devised a system of internal control by assigning students in each department a supervisory role over those in the one just below them.

What passes now for student activities strongly resembled the patriotic and educational work one might find in the immigrant Polish parish. The first and for long the flagship student organization was the St. Casimir (Polish) Literary Society. Founded in 1896 as the "Sons of Poland Society" by two classics students, Peter Budnik and Joseph Strauss, it produced plays and musicales, sponsored debates and literary evenings, and commemorated major Polish national events of the partition era. In the generation before the First World War, long and regular commemorations of the Third of May Constitution, the November Uprising, and the January Insurrection were features of the Polish neighborhood life to which Seminary students were graduated. The Literary Society also built a significant student library and, in 1900, produced the first student periodical, *Głos Studenta (Student Voice),* handwritten and mimeographed in Polish. The St. Cecilia Club came into being in 1902 to support the Seminary's music program, by then including a symphony orchestra founded in 1890 and a choir in 1898.

Daily student life in an urban, mostly boarding school environment differed from that made familiar later in the isolated, rural, boarding school atmosphere of Orchard Lake. Still, some precedents were set in Detroit: "strict discipline and a strenuous program," as a later historian put it. The day ran from 5:30 a.m. to 10:00 p.m. Classes were held from eight in the morning to noon and from two to four in the afternoon, Monday to Wednesday, Friday and Saturday. Thursday, a half-day, and holidays were taken up with excursions to Belle Isle or in the nearby country. The Felician sisters, who lived a block away, kept house and cooked at the Seminary. Competitive sports, which offered major relief from the schedule, were well-developed by 1900 when the Seminary had three baseball teams, a highly successful soccer team, a boxing program and, sporadically, a football team. Baseball was the ruling passion during the immigrant era. Outfitted with "white suits, red socks, red insignia 'PS' on the shirts and caps, bats, masks, gloves, etc."—all donated by their patron Father Francis Mueller, an alumnus and pastor at St. Albertus—the team was a frequent Polish-American challenger to the Jesuit (and Irish) Detroit College (later the University of Detroit), Assumption College in Windsor, and the Michigan Military Academy in Orchard Lake.[21]

The recruitment of a faculty to implement the program of the Seminary posed special problems. Qualified Polish priest-professors were even scarcer than priests for parishes. Several religious communities were mentioned as sources of staff and an academic tradition. Only Polish Jesuits were considered seriously. None came forward, however; and the first rectors recruited as best they could through Polish bishops (Dąbrowski's first plan), Roman contacts, and from among immigrant and native laymen. Until the 1920s, the faculty of the schools had a provisional character. Diocesan clergy from Poland usually had the requisite credentials, but they consistently used an appointment at the Seminary as an entré to pastoral work in America. Only Rev. Witold Buhaczkowski, of the priests whom Dąbrowski recruited this way, remained more than five years.

Alumni priests offered more hope of faculty stability, but

just three, Rev. John Mueller, a member of the Seminary's charter class, Rev. Leon Jarecki, and Rev. John Godrycz, returned to teach for more than five years during the first generation. Several showed promise of creating an academic tradition at the Seminary. Father Mueller was a principal editor of *Niedziela (Sunday)*, the Seminary's newspaper. Father Godrycz, for example, published *Essays on the Foundation of Education* in 1900, but left the Seminary after the student rebellion of 1903. Dąbrowski himself was well-known for his textbooks and spiritual writings.

Paradoxically, lay faculty, who taught for the most part in the classics department, committed more of their careers to the Seminary. They also established the scholarly credentials of the Seminary in the minds of the nationalist Polish intelligentsia. Romuald Piątkowski, the earliest of them, joined the faculty in 1892. His translation of Immanuel Kant's *Prolegomena to Metaphysics* was published in Warsaw in 1901. Thomas Siemiradzki, born like Piątkowski in the Russian partition, came to the United States as a lecturer on Polish history under the aegis of the Polish National Alliance in 1896 and remained as an instructor in classical languages at the Seminary. Sophisticated, noble, and anti-Russian, Siemiradzki collaborated with Piątkowski in promoting the PNA's organization in Detroit. Before leaving Detroit in 1901, to edit *Zgoda (Harmony)*, the organ of the PNA in Chicago, he completed the first volume of his *Post-Partition History of Poland*.

Siemiradzki's successor on the faculty, Ignatius Machnikowski, held degrees from the universities in Kraków and Breslau. Engineer, medical doctor, author, and master of at least fourteen languages, he taught at the Seminary until 1933. Andrew Piwowarski, who came to teach classical languages in 1903, held a law degree from the Jagiellonian University in Kraków and compiled the first histories of the Seminary for its 25th and 50th anniversaries. He left in 1912 to join Piątkowski, who had been named first rector of the PNA's new Alliance College in Cambridge Springs, Pennsylvania. The circle of major lay Polish teachers was completed with Peter Łobaza, instructor in Polish and history from 1911 to 1941, and Andrew Martusiewicz from 1913 to 1943. Several early "American" teachers of English also remained with the schools for substantial periods of time: among them, Joseph Weber from 1898 to 1910, and Allen Campbell (who was also the Seminary's attorney) from 1907 to 1915.

Financing the Polish Seminary was not a simple task. Tuition during the Dąbrowski era was $150 per year, but it is doubtful if the school collected more than half the amount owed it. Needy students were not turned away, and tuition was frequently remitted or deferred. Of necessity Father Dąbrowski showed considerable ingenuity in raising money. The appeals which marked the founding of the Seminary continued. Bequests (Father Moczygemba's was the first large one in 1891) and gifts from Polonian associations and clerics were important if irregular sources of income. The Seminary held its first fair and raffle in 1892. The short-lived Alumni Association of 1899 may have lent a hand also. Donations in kind—books from bishops or food from the larder of the Felician Motherhouse—nourished mind and body directly. A printery, a bookstore and the popular newspaper, *Niedziela,* earned steady profits.

Conflict within Polonia prevented the Seminary from realizing the full potential for financial support. The construction of St. Albertus and the parochial tension, which had hampered initial construction in 1884-1886, took new form in 1888 when Father Kolasiński returned from exile in the Dakota Territory to build another base in Sweetest Heart of Mary parish. Dąbrowski took a more neutral pose in public this time, but the memory of his part in ousting Kolasiński from St. Albertus in 1885 put him in a bad light with people who wanted Poles to control their own church affairs. Probably, the temperaments of the two priests and Dąbrowski's loyalty to his bishop had more to do with the antagonism between them and their supporters than ideological differences. After 1894, when the threatened schism at Sweetest Heart was healed through the intervention of the Apostolic Delegate, they patched things up between them. Kolasiński went so far as to accept an ordinand from the Seminary as an assistant shortly before he died in 1898. Characteristically, the pastor celebrated the occasion in style with a banquet for the Seminary faculty. Two weeks later Dąbrowski led the delegation of priests to his old rival's funeral mass.

Whether by design or accident, Dąbrowski aligned himself with the Polish National Alliance in its bitter struggle for influence in Polonia with the Polish Roman Catholic Union of America from 1886 through the 1890s. The PRCUA, dominated by the Resurrectionists and Father Vincent Barzyński, took the view that "there are only as many good Poles as there are good Catholics" while the PNA, a lay organization with significant clerical support, took a pluralistic view of Polish culture, holding that Poles were mainly, but by no means exclusively, Roman Catholic. When Dąbrowski appealed to the PNA for support, the conventions of 1887 and 1891 responded by assessing the membership. Father Barzyński was deeply hurt by the apparent disloyalty of his former colleague, and a similar appeal to the PRCUA in 1893 was rejected because the Seminary was "a private institution and Father Dąbrowski had never as yet personally petitioned the Catholic Union for help."[22] The Polish Roman Catholic Association of Detroit, which broke away from the PRCUA in 1896, later made up for the refusal of its parent organization to help.

Earlier, in 1890, Father Dąbrowski had tried to stake out a neutral position in Polonia's intramural conflicts: "Since the Seminary does not belong to any party, no one can accuse us of partisanship; we allow everyone freedom of judgement and viewpoint; the doors and heart of the Seminary are always open to every upright Polish priest without exception. We are always grateful to our benefactors and forgive our enemies and pray for them."[23] No matter how he explained it, however, Dąbrowski was accused of consorting with the Masons, Jews, socialists, atheists, and anarchists who were alleged to influence the PNA. On the other hand, there were frequent complaints from its so-called allies that the Seminary took Polish money but that it was the property either of Dąbrowski or a non-Polish bishop who failed to account for the contributions of hard-working Poles. When the Seminary staunchly defended the authority of the Catholic bishops against schismatic Poles in the late 1890s, many of its critics took it as confirmation of those complaints.

The very inconsistency of the complaints demonstrated how Dąbrowski was compelled to steer a course between the American bishops upon whom the Seminary depended for its life and those who questioned the purity of its Polish Catholic soul. He was confronted as he had been in other ways since 1870 with the dilemma of what it meant in practice to be Polish-American in the immigrant era. That may account for the passive role played by the Seminary in the campaign for a Polish-American bishop. The drive for *równouprawnienie,* or equality of right in the American Catholic hierarchy, became, after 1900, the core response of Polish Roman Catholic priests to the charge of the schismatics that Poles had no voice in the Church they were expected to support. When, in 1903, the Polish-American clergy were asked for their preferences in a bishop, they chose men involved in urban parish work. The new rector, Witold Buhaczkowski placed eighth in the poll, receiving only 33 votes out of 419 cast. None of the school's alumni and only one former faculty member, Father Michael Barabasz (vice-rector in 1890-1892) who placed fourth, were considered for a post eventually filled by Rev. Paul Rhode as Auxiliary Bishop of Chicago in 1908.

The Seminary, of course, had ways of presenting its case to Polonia. *Niedziela,* founded in 1891 to defend and publicize the Seminary, was widely read. The PNA granted scholarships to Seminary students; and *Zgoda,* under the editorship of Thomas Siemiradzki, gave the Seminary a good press. The Seminary associated itself closely with the protest in Prussia against the imposition of German as the language of religious instruction in 1901. On the whole, however, it took a less nationalist tone and a more positive attitude toward the wishes of the American bishops than many Polish-American Catholic activists would have liked after 1900.

Father Dąbrowski twice considered incorporation to

relieve doubts about the financial management of the institution and to guarantee its Polish character. He preferred to achieve this as a pontifical seminary under the jurisdiction of the Congregation for the Propagation of the Faith as the German-American Seminary, the Josephinum in Columbus, Ohio, had done in 1888. When Cardinal Ledochowski, by then the Prefect of the Propaganda, refused this request, Dąbrowski worked out a plan in which the Bishop of Detroit held title to the property and chaired the corporation which controlled the Seminary. The plan was put aside in 1894 or 1895, possibly because of a proposal in Rome to give management of the Seminary to a community of friars. About a year later, in 1896, the New Yorker, Erasmus Jerzmanowski, Polonia's first millionaire, reportedly stimulated a second effort to incorporate. He seems to have offered to endow the Seminary if it reported its financial affairs publicly and vested ownership in a board of Polish clerical and lay leaders. His plan also failed to be realized, possibly because of fears of undue lay control over an ecclesiastical institution.

The administrative structure of the Seminary during the immigrant era remained simple. It was the property of the diocese of Detroit, and the rector was legally a diocesan official responsible to the Catholic Bishop of Detroit. As a matter of fact, Bishops Borgess, Foley, and Gallagher allowed the early rectors full freedom to administer the Seminary. Their style was essentially pastoral and paternal—a mixture of affection for their charges and a stern, reserved, authoritarian outward demeanor.

When Dąbrowski retired from teaching in 1896 to concentrate on his chaplaincy to the Felician Sisters, he also delegated routine administrative responsibility to a vice-rector, Father Witold Buhaczkowski at first and Father John Mueller in 1900. Probably it was Mueller's rigidity and inattention, as well as recurrent crowding and neglect of physical facilities, that allowed student unrest to develop into a "strike" in January, 1903. Mueller was the principle object of criticism in the petition of philosophers and theologians who demanded his removal. The specific complaints reflected careless administration—inferior food and laundry service, severe and ineffective discipline, the failure to hire a professor of liturgy or to appoint a spiritual director, and failure to insure the status of the seminarians (both philosophers and theologians) *vis-á-vis* the classics (today's high school) students. Perhaps the rebels had justice and the neighboring community on their side, but in Dąbrowski's mind the issue was obedience and the authority of the church. When the petitioners refused to apologize promptly, 29 of them—a majority of the seminary department—were expelled. Less than three weeks later, on February 15, 1903, Dąbrowski, weakened by stress and influenza, suddenly died. There were other casualties of the student protest. Two faculty members, Fathers John Godrycz and John Moneta, were rumored to have inspired the petition and left the Seminary at the end of the school year. At least half the expelled students were ordained from other seminaries, their success diminishing the reputation of the Polish Seminary.

Dąbrowski's successor, Father Witold Buhaczkowski quickly assumed responsiblilty for every detail of administration, faculty recruitment, fund-raising, and maintenance. His inspections of students for physical cleanliness were legendary. A short cough, rattling keys, and a little Boston terrier announced him on his daily inspection of the Seminary quarters. A graduate of the Gregorian University, Buhaczkowki had been a major voice in the Seminary almost since its beginning. As a voracious reader and a scholar, he insisted on a high standard of student performance in the classroom and worked diligently to recruit good faculty. His stubbornness, nervous habits, and obsession with physical cleanliness may not have been marks of an ideal administrator, but his daring gamble on the future assured his reputation and the survival of the Seminary in the long-run.

Increasingly, the schools found themselves crowded by neighborhood development in Detroit. The completion in 1905 of a chapel wing begun by Dąbrowski and the addition of a classroom-gymnasium building on Garfield Avenue early in 1909 rounded off the original construction plan but only partially relieved the accumulated pressure of 300 boarding and day students and 20 resident faculty. The decision to purchase the grounds and buildings of the Michigan Military Academy, about twenty-five miles to the northwest in Orchard Lake, solved the problem at a stroke. The move had been considered for some time; but it still came as a shock, delighting the 100 students who forfeited an away baseball game to rush back to Detroit to confirm the press report. Having played against the Cadets of the Academy, they knew what to expect at the Lake. People in the St. Albertus neighborhood were disappointed, a feeling that turned into a sense of betrayal of Polish interests when the diocese refused to donate or sell the buildings at less then value to the parish which believed it had done the most to erect them.

On July 20-21, 1909, the equipment and furnishings of the Military Academy were put up for auction, while in Detroit, students and faculty packed Seminary furnishings and personal belongings onto open flat cars. Eleven times, in July and August, between 2:00 and 4:00 A.M., they moved the pieces of their material world directly and without charge over electric street car lines into another country.

Rev. Leopold Moczygemba's petition to Pope Leo XIII, January 14, 1879, explaining the need for a Polish Seminary in America and asking for permission to collect funds for that purpose. The Pope gives his assent at the end of the letter.

Beatissimo Padre.

Il Padre Leopoldo Moczygemba dell'Ordine Dei Minori Conventuali, Missionario Apostolico negli Stati Uniti dell'America Settentrionale, e presentemente per poco tempo Penitenziere in San Pietro per la lingua Inglese, prostrato al bacio del Sacro Piede, umilmente espone alla V.S., che, siccome nell'America vi sono più di ducento mila Polacchi, sparsi per diversi stati, e li mancano sufficienti Sacerdoti della stessa nazione pei loro spirituali bisogni, che sono grandi, egli intende di stabilire un Seminario per la gioventù della medesima nazione che si dedicherà alla via ecclesiastica, e siccome egli deve cominciare colle proprie sue limosine ed il resto spera in ajuto di Dio e nella pietà dei fedeli, perciò supplica la V.S. a degnarsi benignamente concedergli la facoltà di

poter spendere a tal scopo tutte le
sue limosine che presentamente possiede e tutto quel che potrà avere
nell'avvenire.
Che etc.

Alla Sua Santità
Leone XIII
felicemente regnante

"Ex aedibus Vaticanis 14 Jan. 1879"
— Annuimus in omnibus —
iuxta petita.
Leo PP. XIII

Left: Rev. Leopold Moczygemba as a young priest, about 1854. Below: The architect's conception of the Polish Seminary building in Detroit in 1885.

Above: Rev. Joseph Dąbrowski, first rector of the Polish Seminary from 1885 to 1903, in the garden of the Felician Sisters' Motherhouse in Detroit. Below: Composite portrait of the faculty and students in the theology program in 1898-1899.

Left: A home in the Polish neighborhood of Detroit early in the twentieth century. Below: The Seminary as it appeared about 1907 after the construction of the chapel wing.

NIEDZIELA

TYGODNIK ILLUSTROWANY DLA LUDU POLSKIEGO W AMERYCE.

Nr. 6.   DETROIT, MICH., 11-go PAŹDZIERNIKA 1891 ROKU.   ROK 1.

Redaktor. Ks. Dr. Mieczysław Barabasz.

KALENDARZYK TYGODNIOWY.			Listy i przedpłatę	PRZEDPŁATA WYNOSI:			
11	Paździe.	N.	Gereona z to.MM.	WYSYŁAĆ NALEŻY POD ADRESEM:	W Stanach Zjedn.		
12	,,	P.	Maxymiliana B.	The Polish Weekly		Rocznie	Półr. Kwart.
13	,,	W	Edwarda Kr.	„NIEDZIELA"		$2.00	$1.00 50 c.
14	,,	Ś.	Kalixta Pap.	DETROIT, MICH.			
15	,,	C.	Jadwigi Wd.	POLISH SEMINARY,	W Austryi.	5 złr.	2.50złr. 1.25.
16	,,	P.	Teresy P.	Cor. St. Aubin and Garfield Ave's.	W Niemczech.	10 mk.	5 mk. 2.50
17	,,	S.	W.ktora B.				

Rękopisów drobniejszych Redakcya nie zwraca.

MARYA—KRÓLOWA POLSKI.

KOCHAJ BOGA I POLSKĘ!   SYNU, I AMERYKĘ KOCHAJ!

MATKI! OJCOWIE!

MÓWCIE Z DZIEĆMI PO POLSKU!!!

Cover page of an early issue of Niedziela (Sunday). *It synthesizes the Seminary's early educational mission under the patronage of "Mary—Queen of Poland": "Love God and Poland! Son, Love America Also! Mothers! Fathers! Speak to your Children in Polish!!!"*

The composite portrait of the graduates of the classics program in 1909, with flags illustrating their Polish and American heritage.

*Right: The Polish Seminary Football Team of 1895.
Below: The Polish Seminary Band in 1907, with Rev. Witold Buhaczkowski, Rector from 1903 to 1916, seated to the right of the director, Professor Francis Górzelniaski.*

Above: Rev. Witold Buhaczkowski with classics faculty and second-year students about 1907. Below: A class in session at the Detroit Seminary.

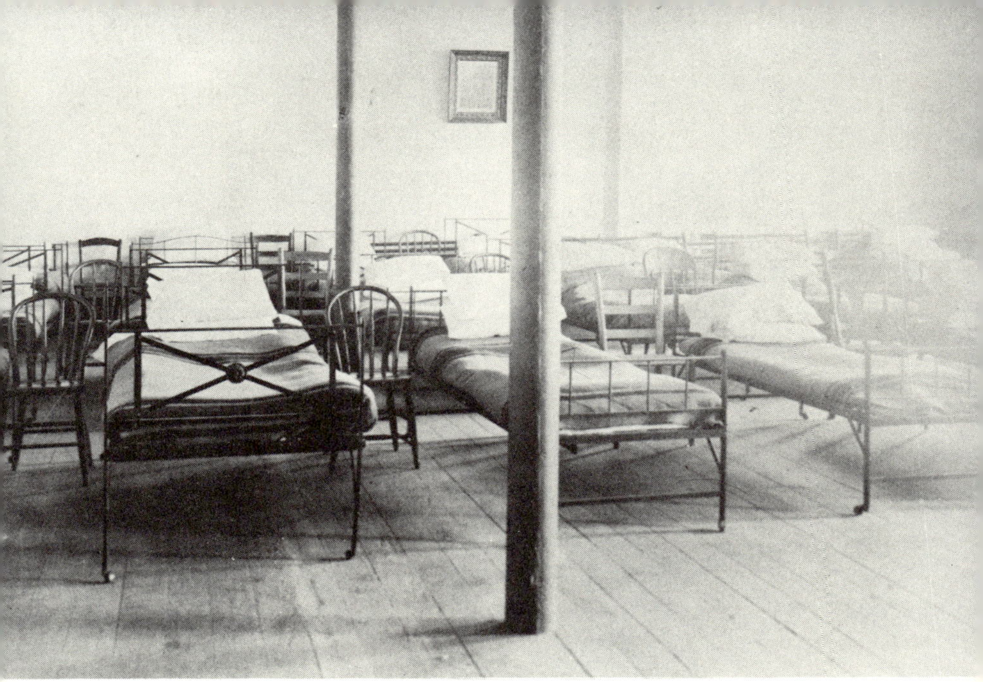

Above: A dormitory in the Detroit Seminary. *Below:* The kitchen in the Detroit Seminary.

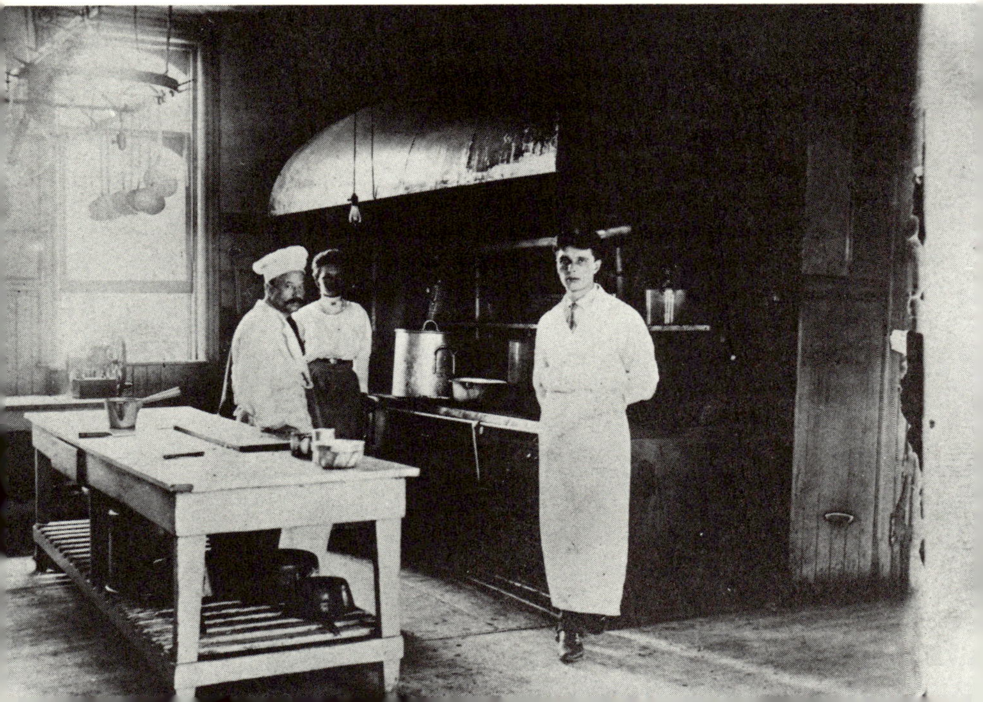

III. *The Polish-American Seminary, 1909-1942*

AMERICA came of age in the first quarter of the twentieth century. The heavy industry Polish immigrants had helped to build was in place and mature, and some sectors, New England textiles and Pennsylvania hard coal, for example, that Poles had done so much to sustain, fell victim to structural economic change in the 1920s. Production for new forms of mass consumption like automobiles and electrical appliances became the cutting edge of economic growth. Meanwhile, managers took control from the free-wheeling, entrepreneurial capitalists who had built American industry. Their techniques of control, organization, and corporate bureaucracy reached down to the factory floor through time-motion studies, assembly-line production, and foremen trained to respond to managerial direction.

The idealism and concern for a better world which had also flavored the first decades of the century gave way to the disillusion and concern for self associated with the jazz age. Immigration restriction, which sought to protect workers from the competition of cheap foreign labor and society from racial contamination by the peoples of eastern and southern Europe, was a historic departure from the belief in America's capacity to absorb, transform, and improve the peoples of the world. As the stream of immigrants dried up in the 1920s, the Polish community increasingly became a second-generation ethnic society.

Polish-Americans also retreated in their own way from social and political idealism in the post-war years. Having contributed to the cherished goal of restoring the Polish state, they found themselves disappointed by the political and economic disarray into which the homeland soon fell. Few immigrants returned to the new Poland. The overwhelming majority committed themselves to life in America and turned inward toward the issues of Polish-Americans.

Detroit was transformed in the early years of the century by automobile manufacture from a medium-sized city of small factories into one of the world's capitals of the new mass production, consumer-oriented economy. The city attracted Polish workers in ever greater numbers from other parts of the United States like the distressed hard coal mining districts of northeastern Pennsylvania, New York, and the farms and copper mines of Michigan. Together with the immigrants who had surged into the city from Austrian and Russian Poland in the decade prior to the First World War, they made Polish-Americans the largest ethnic group in Detroit and Detroit the most Polish-American of the large Polonias. Between 1900 and 1914, the city's Polish population more than doubled from 48,000 to at least 110,000. The east and west side corridors of Polish settlement grew out rapidly along lines established in the 1880s. By 1925, the locus of east side Polonia was the densely populated enclave of Hamtramck, no more than a village amid farmlands at the turn of the century.

The great Dodge Main plant, straddling the boundary of Detroit and Hamtramck, eventually employed 20,000 mostly Polish workers. It and other citadels of assembly-line production gave a more pronounced working class character to Detroit Polonia after 1910. They also generated the income to create new neighborhoods and at least a dozen new Polish Catholic parishes between the wars. As families found work for younger and new immigrant members in their shops, the new factories served as guarantors of kinship as well as of community. Fraternal insurance associations expanded rapidly as they found new ways to incorporate women and children into their ranks. In the aftermath of the First World War and the liberation of Poland, the fraternals and other community groups reoriented themselves to the needs of Polish-Americans and embarked upon the long process of defining the Polish-American identity. The parish, press, and organizational network of Polish-America reached its greatest extent in the late 1920s, as the children of the immigrants, the second generation, expanded the demographic base on which that network rested.

Wages were good in the auto plants when there was work. But employment was cyclic; speed-ups were frequent; and the arbitrary power of foremen was a frequent source of dissatisfaction. Lay-offs were common during model changeovers or as demand slackened, and occasional economic shocks like the brief depressions of 1913-1914 and 1920-1921 threatened to wipe out the gains of years of effort. Economic recoveries did not eliminate the poverty and social problems related to increased dependence on unskilled labor and cyclic consumer demand. The Great Depression of the 1930s finally deprived many Poles of the jobs and homes on which they had built their communities. The response shaped a generation. What had been an interesting but small radical labor movement in the 1920s was upstaged by the successful organizing drives of the United Automobile Workers from 1937 to 1941. As pillars of the UAW and the New Deal Democratic political coalition, Polish-Americans worked their way back from poverty to security and laid the social groundwork for the advances of the third and fourth generations after the Second World War.

The Polish Seminary only seemed remote from the transformations of the community of its birth. True, the move to Orchard Lake in 1909 had liberated the Seminary from many of the physical and social constraints of the immigrant neighborhood. It was not without its problems, however. The purchase price of the Michigan Military

Academy was a bargain at $83,000—the founder's widow had been offered $250,000 for the property a few years earlier—but Father Buhaczkowski was able to put down only $33,000 at first. He had hoped to sell the old property on St. Aubin to make up the rest; but the most likely purchaser, St. Albertus' parish, was unwilling to offer enough. Indeed, the parishioners, led by Rev. Francis Mueller, believed the whole property should have given to them in light of their earlier contributions to the Seminary. Instead, the Rector secured two loans of $25,000 each, a debt which was lifted in 1912 when all the Seminary's old assets were sold to a cigar manufacturing company for $40,500. When the main building was razed some twenty years later, several priests from Orchard Lake salvaged the well-lodged cornerstone and some bricks from the wreckage for the new campus where they now form the base of the Founders Monument. Only the classroom-gymnasium building of 1908, used for a while by St. Albertus School, remains at the corner of St. Aubin and Garfield. Dąbrowski Field, the vacant lot where the Seminary once stood, now bears silent and lonely witness to its Polish Catholic heritage.

Orchard Lake posed more than a sharp physical contrast to St. Albertus' neighborhood. Located in the heart of Michigan's lake district, it was, by 1909, a refuge for summer vacationers from Detroit. Comfortable interurban railways, automobiles, and the Grand Trunk Railway put Orchard Lake in easy contact with Detroit and any other place in the Midwest. Summer automobile traffic was such a nuisance finally that local leaders joined the third Rector, Father Grupa, to incorporate the village of Orchard Lake in 1928, mainly to protect the community from its unregulated intrusion. By then, the Seminary had settled in. When it had arrived in 1909, it took possession of eight substantial buildings in a variety of Gothic and Romanesque revival styles. They were bare of furnishings, spare of utilities, and a less than perfect match with the numbers and purposes of the students and faculty.

The oldest of the acquisitions, the Castle, had already led three lives: from 1858 to 1872 as the grand residence of lawyer, businessman, general, and judge, Joseph T. Copeland; from 1872 to 1877 as a much expanded resort hotel under a partnership of Copeland and some Pontiac investors; and from 1879, as the first all-purpose building of the Michigan Military Academy and later the home of its commander, Colonel Joseph Rogers. The Seminary continued the tradition by first using the Castle as chapel, canteen, and living quarters for professors. The Barracks, built by Rogers about 1881, were a rectangular set of six contiguous units and served as dormitories for the seminarians as they had for the cadets of the Academy. The Class Building, at a right angle to the Barracks, housed ten classrooms, the library, and a biology laboratory on the first two stories and the Classics Chapel on the third.

The Gymnasium was easily the most versatile of the buildings at the start. When the school year opened in 1909, 350 students were present to live in quarters designed for 144 cadets. Their number grew to 461 in four years. The Gymnasium was quickly fitted out as a dormitory for the classics students with beds on the main floor and on the raised running track which circled the interior. The basement held indoor sinks and the only shower facilities on campus. A flooded basement, failure in plumbing, or frozen pipes drove everyone to one of the few pumps on campus or in good weather to the lake itself. The old Quartermaster's Building, now the Administration Building, housed the Rector's office and apartment, the student infirmarian's apartment, and the Orchard Lake Post Office (on the ground floor), an infirmary and faculty apartments (on the second floor) and music rooms (in the rear of the ground floor). The Dining Hall, adjacent to the Administration Building, was much larger than its descendants (the Classics Chapel, later the Galeria) owing to the kitchen, bakery, and ice house in the rear. Across from the Dining Hall, toward the lake, the first faculty residence (formerly the home of Col. Rogers' son) housed most of the instructors.

The first building priority was living quarters for students. In 1912, the old Riding Arena, now the Activities Building, was converted into a combined Classics dormitory (the second floor), classroom, study hall, and library facility (the first floor). Between 1914 and 1916, a three-story Seminary residence building with chapel was erected for $35,000 to house the philosophy and theology students.

The work of adapting the Academy's facilities to the Seminary's needs continued apace after Buhaczkowski's retirement to Italy in 1916. During a snowy night in January, 1917, the kitchen wing of the Dining Hall caught fire and burned. The Pontiac Fire Department was unable to pass through the blocked roads and, in the purest Orchard Lake tradition, Father Arnold Waszyca, a spiritual director, led a band of students in tearing down the walls between the kitchen and the main dining room, which they saved. This disaster, which ushered in Father Grupa's rectorship in 1917, set several changes in motion. What was left of the Dining Hall was converted into the campus Chapel, later the Classics Chapel. The first floor of the Classics (now the Activities) Building became the refectory, the renowned "Gulashville," for nearly a half-century. A new Classics Building with 23 dormitories, recreation room, canteen, and three study-lecture halls was opened in 1924 at a cost of $60,000. Immediately dubbed "Noah's Ark" in memory of an unfinished skylight from which "doves" could escape and in recognition of its patriarchal social arrangement, it too became an intensely personal landmark to generations of students.

The final major project in the first building era was the reconstruction of the Barracks from 1926 to 1928 for $175,000. The entire front was demolished to make space for a corridor and a new section of rooms running the length of the building. A student dormitory wing was added at the south end in 1926 and a faculty wing at the north end in 1928. The new housing was meant primarily to accommodate the lower division of the college level student population, then emerging as a more distinct entity. It was possible now to open the second and third floors of the Faculty Residence to a dozen or so "select and favored few" collegians. Their special status freed them somewhat from close supervision—it was easier, for example, to listen to one's own radio—and anticipated the social spirit of the building when it was known as the "Frat" house in the early 1930s. When the Felician Sisters arrived on campus in 1935, it was transformed once more, this time into a convent.

During the mid-twenties, before the financial panic of 1929 and the Great Depression put an end to all such work, a number of physical amenities made the campus more attractive and usable. An eighteen car garage and two equipment rooms were erected behind the Administration Building; an imposing entrance gate opened the west side of the campus to Indian Trail; a print shop was established on the first floor of the Class Building; and the Classics Chapel was given a balcony, a rear entrance, and an annex housing a sacristy and a separate area with four side altars.

Along with the academic and residential buildings, the Seminary also acquired from the military academy a seventy acre farm which supplied much of its food. For years, homegrown root vegetables, cabbages, corn, grapes, apples, cherries, peaches, plums, and pears were staples of the Orchard Lake diet long into the winter as the kitchen drew upon fresh and preserved stores in the basement of the Gymnasium. Poultry, chicken, brooder, and pig houses guaranteed a year round supply of eggs or of meat, especially at holiday times. Barns for cows and, until they were replaced by tractors, Belgian-style horses were also part of the village landscape.

The leadership at Orchard Lake, as well as the physical contrast with Detroit, revealed the process of Polish-Americanization that dominated the development of the Seminary between the World Wars. Fathers Dąbrowski and Buhaczkowski, reared in Poland and educated in Rome, had imprinted an immigrant Polish Catholicism and Roman loyalism upon the Seminary. The accuracy of their perception of what should be done was reflected in the success of what they did. When Buhaczkowski resigned for reasons of health in 1916, he presided over the most substantial enterprise in higher education in American Polonia. His immediate successors, who consolidated that achievement in the post-immigrant era, had significantly different biographies. All but one (Rev. Anthony Kłowo) were reared in the United States, and all were educated at least in part at Orchard Lake.

Rev. Michael Grupa, who ushered in the ethnic, Polish-American era as rector from 1917 to 1932, was brought to America as an infant and reared in Minnesota. He took the classics program in the old building on St. Aubin Street and completed philosophy and theology at the Seminary in St. Paul and at various European universities. His was an example of the relative speed with which Polish immigrants produced a native clergy. His case may have owed something to Archbishop John Ireland of St. Paul who, though he respected the strength of ethnic identities, foresaw their merging into a common American Catholic culture. An American trained clergy was indispensable to that process. When he delivered this message at the Seminary in Detroit in 1898, Ireland caused a stir in the Polish press; by 1916, it seemed less of an issue. Father Grupa was serving then as a pastor in Omaha when Bishop Paul Rhode, the unofficial spiritual leader of Polish-Americans, recommended his appointment as rector. When he succeeded Buhaczkowski early in 1917, Grupa was only 31 years old, fitted by age as well as background to meet the challenge within Polonia presented by the emergence of an ethnic or Polish-American generation in the 1920s and 1930s. A sophisticated and skilled speaker with an imposing physical presence, he became a popular lecturer at the Jesuit University of Detroit. In an era of renowned priest-orators, Grupa's talents commanded large audiences throughout the region.

Father Grupa's two immediate successors, men with different personalities and backgrounds, both joined the faculty during his tenure. Rev. Anthony Kłowo (rector in 1932-1937) emigrated to America at 22 and completed his studies for the priesthood at the Polish Seminary before a stint of pastoral work in Chicago. Returning to the Lake in 1919, he devoted his considerable energies and organizational talents to the schools until his death in 1937. Rev. Ladislaus Krzyżosiak, the fifth rector, was born in Pennsylvania and completed classics and philosophy at Orchard Lake. Soon after ordination in 1923, he joined the faculty as instructor in mathematics and physics and held a number of administrative posts, chiefly Dean of the College under Kłowo. His administration (1937-1943) consolidated changes initiated in the Grupa era through reincorporation and a stronger relationship with Polonia.

There was no manifesto by which Grupa announced the changes of the 1920s, but their outline is clear. The only continuing administrator under Buhaczkowski had been a registrar. Early in Grupa's time, two major central offices were created, Procurator-Treasurer and Secretary-General, and the administration of the schools was somewhat decentralized by the appointment of a principal and dean of discipline for classics and deans of discipline for the Seminary's upper (theology) and lower (philosophy) divisions. Under the European system, which prevailed during the immigrant era, the College lacked any identity. What would have been its first or second years, in American terms, was part of the classics program. Its third and fourth years, called philosophy after its major course of study, were preliminary to the Seminary's theology program.

The possibility that accrediting agencies might force redefinition of all non-seminary education as a high school was a real one. The Resurrectionists' St. Stanislaus "College" in Chicago, for one, had been compelled to redefine itself realistically as Weber High School. At Orchard Lake the classics department had been certified in 1915 as St. Mary's High School by the Michigan Department of Education, and a college identity began to emerge clearly in the decade that followed. Whatever the exact reason, it seemed natural that the curricular and administrative structure should evolve, as recommended by two consultant deans from the University of Michigan in 1927, in the direction of the American system. In that year, the trend toward separating levels of education was confirmed formally with the creation of three departments, each with four year programs: St. Mary's High School, St. Mary's College, and SS. Cyril and Methodius Seminary. The reorganization effectively put the theology program of the Seminary on the graduate level. In the College, however, the distinction between upper and lower divisions perpetuated something of the old pull toward classics and theology. The perception that the College had emerged from the High School—that it was really a junior college—was borne out by the practice of holding joint College-High School commencements in the 1930s, and, in 1937, when St. Mary's received junior college accreditation from the National Catholic Education Association. The emphasis on the philosophy program in the upper division made the last two years seem simply like a preparation for the Seminary.

Organization into three departments was followed by further administrative changes. The office of vice-rector was revived, and deans of studies were appointed in the College and Seminary. An administrative board in the College and academic councils in each department guaranteed a strong consultative role for the faculties of the three schools. During the 1930s, the faculty even asserted some control over administration by nominating candidates for various offices. When Edward Mooney became Archbishop of Detroit, he restored a measure of hierarchical authority at Orchard Lake by appointing several new administrators in 1938 and by filling the new post of vice-president of the College with Rev. Joseph Gierut, the dean of studies.

Administrative change also entailed curriculum reform, chiefly in the College. There, a philosophy sequence founded on scholasticism was the core of an enriched curriculum including courses in teacher education, mathematics, languages, science, social sciences, elocution, and Gregorian chant. It was now possible to offer Bachelor's Degrees in Arts, Science, and Philosophy. The written theses required in the majors demonstrated a wide range of intellectual interests in both students and their mentors. They also highlighted the limitations of the curriculum. According to the visiting accreditation team from the North Central Association of Colleges and Secondary Schools in 1941, "these theses furnish the only striking evidence of developed student initiative, every other aspect of scholarly endeavor being characterized by prescribed procedures."[1] They also reveal a narrow range of majors. For the most part, and entirely so after 1936-1937, the theses fell in the areas of Polish literature, Polish-American history, and philosophy.

The difficulty of offering more than two coherent majors (philosophy and Polish) encouraged lay students to withdraw after their second year in the College. The absence of students at the senior college level in turn made it difficult to sustain the majors which would have fostered both retention and recruitment. Students who attempted to transfer to other schools found they could obtain no more than high school credit for their college work while students who wished to transfer to the College had little incentive to do so. After years of discussion, the administration decided to break out of this circular problem by seeking accreditation from the North Central Association in 1941. Given the emphasis that North Central put on the quantitative measurement of institutional achievement, the effort was bound to fail. In any case, accreditation seemed less relevant at a moment when the College was reorienting itself entirely toward a divinity school.

The High School and Seminary curricula, largely prescribed by the regulations of the State of Michigan or by canon law for the education of priesthood candidates, changed little except that some courses were shaved off each and added to the College program. The major changes revolved around the language of instruction. English gradually replaced Polish as a classroom language after the 1920s, and the Seminary introduced formal courses in Polish and Polish homiletics to sharpen a declining native ability in the language among its students. College senior theses, frequently written in Polish in the early 1930s, were almost all in English after 1939.

The Grupa administration, with strong support from Bishop Michael Gallagher, Mooney's predecessor from 1918 to 1937, also introduced a policy for faculty recruitment and development which lasted until the early 1970s and left its mark long afterward. Fathers Dąbrowski and Buhaczkowski had usually hired mature faculty, both lay and clerical, in Europe and America. Their qualifications varied, and their commitment to the Seminary was seldom long-lasting. Immigrant priests especially used the Seminary as a way station to parish work. Grupa and his successors, on the other hand, built a core of loyal priest-faculty by seeking out promising candidates in the student body and by encouraging and financing them in their studies. Bishop Gallagher cooperated by adopting them for the Diocese of Detroit, so that they might return to Orchard Lake after ordination. They were encouraged to travel and pursue advanced studies, usually through the M.A.; but some, like Fathers Constantine Cyran and Joseph Rybiński, took doctorates as well. Resident priest-faculty were also expected to continue their education with weekend course work at nearby universities. On campus their lives were nearly as regulated as the students' whom they supervised, and except for a few administrators they left for full-time parish work during vacation periods. Throughout the year, they served the Archdiocese on weekends and holy days as preachers, moderators, retreat masters, and teachers.

The student body, which reached a peak of 540 in 1929, was also transformed. Though never an immigrant school, the fact that as many as 40% of the students were Polish-born in the early years gave the Seminary a special flavor. During the 1920s, the number of the foreign-born dwindled into insignificance, and the children of immigrants, the second generation that possessed fluency in a kind of household Polish-American language, dominated the campus. Owing mainly to the size of the High School, lay students were the large majority of residents and graduates. What had been considered temporary in Father Dąbrowski's time had become integral to the schools. The leadership realized, as the North Central team pointed out in 1941, "that the Polish people are willing to support an institution of higher learning but that they probably would not support merely a theological seminary since . . . such an undertaking is largely the responsibility of the various dioceses in which the Polish priests are later on to labor."[2] Polish-Americans found the Lake an acceptable form of transition from immigrant family and neighborhood life into professional and business careers which required dealing with a larger world than they had been born to. Also implicit in the appeal of the schools was their willingness to charge less to bring education within reach of young Polish-Americans. In 1941, for example, the College charged $350 for room, board, and tuition for one year. The schools never rejected an applicant for academic reasons, relying on letters from pastors and principals to judge admissions. They preferred to develop students within a disciplined academic and social life style tempered by the personal counseling expected in a seminary atmosphere. Orchard Lake was prepared academically, culturally, and administratively to fulfill the dreams of immigrant parents for their children.

The curriculum through which students passed operated at two levels: the formal, academic one; and a second curriculum of spiritual, moral, intellectual, and social formation. The distinction between the two was never great in the cloistered residential atmosphere of Orchard Lake. For the sake of the dream immigrants and their children willingly accepted the spare and heavily scheduled style of life devised by Father Buhaczkowski in Detroit and perfected in the seclusion of Orchard Lake. Communications with home were well-regulated by the disciplinarians. Superficially, the cycle of meals, prayer, study, and recreation left no time unaccounted for. Seminarians, who followed a slightly stricter routine than the collegians or high schoolers, set the tone for the campus. They rose at 5:30 a.m. for meditation and mass in the Seminary chapel. Breakfast, eaten in silence at 7:30, was followed by a brief visit to the chapel, and the first class bell at 7:50 announced morning classes from 8:00 to 11:50. Lunch at noon was followed by a period of reading after which conversation was permitted. A visit to the chapel and a recreational hour or nap from 1:00 to 2:00 p.m. constituted the mid-day break. Classes resumed from 2:00 to 4:00 followed by recreation to 5:00, study to 5:40, recitation of the rosary, and dinner from 6:00 to 6:30. A chapel visit, recreation to 7:00, study in silence in one's room until 9:15 and night prayers led to the official conclusion of the day at 10:00 p.m.

College and high school students followed a similar

schedule, except that they rose half an hour later and prayed and napped less. During lunch they were entertained with readings in Polish while underclassmen served the food. Thursdays and Saturdays were only half-days academically. Those afternoons were free for long hikes around Orchard or Pine Lakes. Saturday evenings were reserved for special entertainments for college men. On Sundays and special holidays the students of the three departments began the day a half-hour later and celebrated mass and held evening services jointly. Longer walks off campus, trips to Pontiac, and the occasional home visit were possible on those days in addition to normal study periods, chapel, and meals. All-school programs on May 3rd (the anniversary of the Polish Constitution of 1791) and on the feasts of the Immaculate Conception, St. Casimir, and St. Joseph were usually held in the evening at 7:30. Everyone, faculty and students alike, was required to attend. Corpus Christi was celebrated in the traditional Polish manner with processions to four outdoor altars on campus; St. Nicholas Day with gifts of candy on door knobs; Shrove Tuesday with *pączki* (doughnuts) and *ścierka* (literally a duster), a large cartoon of campus life; Easter with the special, blessed foods of the *święcone* meal; and Easter Monday with the ritualized pranks of *dyngus.*

With a few modifications, the Orchard Lake way of daily life that emerged in the 1920s and 1930s persisted until the 1960s and in some important ways until the 1970s. During the heyday of the system, there was some relaxation of the rules against conversation between members of different departments and receiving gifts from home. The lights-out policy was applied more easily to separate dormitories after the construction of the Ark and the new Barracks decentralized the electrical system. New students at every level and even new faculty were introduced with elaborate initiation ceremonies which communicated expected behavior more effectively than any written rule book. Student and faculty handbooks were not deemed necessary until the 1960s, and even then their contents were treated more as commentary on the "real" body of knowledge passed along orally. As one administrator put it in 1937, when asked to explain the absence of an available, written statement of the policy of sixty-day notice for termination of a faculty contract: "It is traditional."[3]

Despite outwardly strict appearances, generations of students who attended other seminaries recollected that discipline at the Lake was never as strict as at its "American" counterparts. There were, of course, the usual pranks, practically institutionalized over the generations. The moderately Roman official discipline was reflected in the dress code. On campus, seminarians always wore cassocks and birettas, overcoats only on cold days, and regulation black shoes. On their neighborhood walks, however, they were permitted sport jackets as well as visits to simple restaurants in imitation of the younger students who dressed more freely on campus and were slightly freer to move about off campus. More mature students were also fairly free to run some campus operations—the infirmary from 1919 to 1925, the library until 1932, and the print shop—as well as their co-curricular activities. Student residential life was supervised by prefects drawn from the next highest academic level except in the theologate where it was self-policing. Perhaps the single most significant deviation from Roman-American seminary discipline at Orchard Lake was the practice of admitting students before they had been adopted by a diocese.

Spiritual formation in the Seminary continued at the Lake in the manner established by the first rectors in Detroit. Sacramental and prayer life were built into the daily routine and expanded on special days and during the months of October and May. Celebrants and homilists at masses were appointed by the rector, and each priest had to take his turn. Retreats were scheduled for February, and confessions were heard on Fridays at 5:00 p.m. by faculty priests but never by priest-administrators. It is not so easy to tell what kind of life was fostered by these means, though the routine of approved student life provides some evidence of a mixture of values and behavior best described as Polish-American. The language, forms, and norms of American education and church life grew steadily if imperceptibly stonger, not only in the classroom but also in the "voluntary" associations and formational activities in which students socialized outside the more heavily supervised academic and dormitory programs.

Father Joseph Rybiński, a former student who joined the faculty in 1925, authoritatively embodied the "traditional" values of self-discipline and denial in the face of American materialism. The affluence and hedonsim of American youth in the 1920s mocked a peasant-immigrant morality based on the conservation of scarce resources, but the Depression of the thirties seemed to confirm its wisdom. By dint of personality and through a long life, Father Rybiński sought to impose a standard for life which challenged the norms of American youth. The spartan simplicity of his personal life was a living reminder to all, and as Dean of Discipline in the Seminary for forty years and an instructor for over fifty, he was in a position to implement his views.

Externally Christocentric in character at first, formation only gradually associated itself with devotion to the Virgin Mary. Its first stage was represented in 1914 when the Sacred Heart Society erected an iron statue of its patron, facing the main quadrangle, at a cost of $1,000. In 1922, Father Kłowo founded the Eucharistic League as the society's mate (Father Rybiński was its second moderator). Dedicated to adoration, reparation, and reception of Christ in the Eucharist, the League was part of a rising tide of devotion which asserted the distinctively Catholic aspects of the American church. The growth of mission work was another sign of the assertive coming of age of American Catholics. In 1919, two seminarians (and later long-time priest-faculty), Francis Orlik and Ladislaus Krzyżosiak, organized the Polish Students Mission Society. Active in supporting foreign missions and domestic extension work through fund-raising, special campus programs, catechizing, and distributing printed material, the Society reached a peak of activity before the Second World War when it published the *Magnet* (1938-1940), a mimeographed English language periodical, and organized sections in the College and High School.

A seminary often called St. Mary's in spite of its official name needed little encouragement in promoting devotion to the Mother of Jesus. What is remarkable is that it took the

Polish-American generation as long as it did to institutionalize that devotion. In 1919, Father Kłowo, together with future priest-faculty members Constantine Cyran and Joseph Rybiński, refounded the Sodality of the Immaculate Conception under the patronage of St. Aloysius Gonzaga. (It had lapsed after the original founder, Father Waszyca, died in 1917.) Membership was extended to the classics division in the same year through a separate unit under the patronage of the Annunciation of the Blessed Virgin Mary and St. Stanislaus Kostka. The Sodality fostered a strong Marian devotion and had a wide impact. It acted to gentle the behavior of men and fostered certain attitudes: a more respectful (and possibly American) view of women than prevailed in traditional, rural Poland; moral self-discipline, especially sexual, by associating immaculate Mary with the ideal of womanhood; and a spirit of service to humankind as well as to Christ.

The extra-devotional activities of the Sodality—theme contests, plays, hospital visits, and Mother's Day programs —expressed Marian values clearly and publicly. Its first woman of the year award was bestowed on the pioneer Detroit Polish social worker, Clara Świeczkowska. A few years after the founding of the Sodality, in 1925, the Literary Society also restored the Third of May celebration to honor both the liberal Polish constitution of 1791, and Mary, Queen of Poland. The Literary Society also founded *Sodalis Maryański,* the longest lived of all the Seminary's publications. A joint student-faculty effort in Polish, *Sodalis* provided 12,000 subscribers in the mid-twenties with news of the Sodality and encouragement to found similar groups in other parishes. The most visible physical evidence of the progress of Marian devotion was the construction of the Orchard Lake Grotto. Twice between the World Wars, seminarians took up the project but were compelled to defer it for lack of funds. Then, a gift of $5,000 from Josephine Rzeppa of Detroit in 1940, the first major individual gift in the Seminary's history, encouraged the administration to take on the project though the schools were facing a major financial and corporate reorganization. Completed by Christmas,

1941, just off the Indian Trail entrance to the campus, the Grotto attracted a steady stream of visitors and served as a center of campus devotion and commemoration.

The Polish Literary Society continued to exercise intellectual leadership among students during the early years at Orchard Lake. In special programs it celebrated the feasts of St. Casimir, its patron; of Peter Skarga, the Jesuit preacher of the Polish Catholic Reformation; and of Father Dąbrowski, the Seminary's founder. The Society sponsored the second student periodical *Wrzos (Heather)* from 1913 to 1916 as a vehicle for creative writing as well as for reports on the Seminary and its history. It also dominated campus play production and expanded its repertory through translations into Polish as it won a regional reputation with performances at Polish parish halls and National Homes. On the other hand, the pull of American culture and the needs of a more Americanized student body were evident soon after the move to Orchard Lake when the Newman English Literary Society was founded to encourage mastery of the English language through debate and dramatic performances on holidays like Washington's and Lincoln's birthdays.

The Seminary Orchestra, Band, and Choir were quickly reestablished at the Lake and prospered, notably in 1914-1917, when a Conservatory of Music flourished, and again after 1920 with the addition of a Glee Club. The ubiquitous Literary Society also assumed responsibility for the choir in the 1920s. The creation of a college department in 1927 led to the organization of a separate collegiate choir and glee club as well as an orchestra-band which played at athletic events. Very much in the spirit of the Jazz Age, the College's "Happy Five" or "Syncopators" (when they grew to nine) entertained at banquets and films.

During the thirties, interest grew in Gregorian Chant, unashamedly medieval "Catholic Music" in contrast to American "Protestant" church music. The inspiration came from European and American Catholic liturgical leaders early in the twentieth century. Chant took root at Orchard Lake in the Seminary's Liturgical Choir, the forerunner of the Schola Cantorum, under the direction of Father Aloysius

Antochowski. There was no need yet to organize special programs of popular Polish music: the student songbook of the day suggests that it was happening informally. The records are silent as to the performance of the urban cabaret or serious classical music which prevailed in the interwar Poland and which the outer world identified with Polish culture. Their absence suggests the growing gap between modern Polish culture and ethnic Polish-American culture after the First World War. What was emerging here was a Polish-American student folk culture, an interpretation of life at the Lake which mingled folk tunes from Poland with American popular music, Catholic Latin hymns, and occasionally sardonic lyrics.

The athletic program also contributed toward a more Polish-American cultural life. Quite early, it generated a significant number of English language publications: the short-lived *Bludgeon* (1915-1916), which served as a vehicle for student writing on various topics, and the *Lakeside Punch* (1921-1929), the first printed and nearly permanent student periodical. A newspaper titled the *Eagle* revived the idea of a student publication in 1938; but, like its predecessors, it was suspended for financial reasons. Finally, the fraternity Phi Gamma Chi, under its second moderator Father John Buszek, launched the official student journal, *The Lake Oracle,* printed continuously since 1940 (with an interruption in 1943-1944).

Phi Gamma Chi functioned in the College from its founding in 1930 through the 1960s much as the Polish Literary Society had in the Seminary. Involved at one time or another in most aspects of college life, it gave a tone, identity, and social comradeship to the newest of the three schools. With Father Alexander Cendrowski as the first moderator it was organized as the Fellows of Good Cheer for social purposes, a regulated exception to Saturday night's study. Its private and public initiations—replete with rules, mock courts, wooden paddles, and costumes—became a feature of the sports season. Outings of members, jackets and beanies, frat nights, Halloween and Shrove Tuesday parties, and annual varsity nights for athletes brought an element of conventional American college social life to the campus and provided a year round social safety valve. The Fraternity House, the Faculty residence until the expansion of the Barracks, rounded out the image of college life as an informal social center. True to an older Orchard Lake tradition, Phi Gamma Chi also served the campus by contributing to a flourishing dramatic tradition in the 1930s and early 1940s. The High School joined that tradition in 1939-1943 with its Little Theatre Productions in English and Polish under the direction of Rev. Edward Popielarz. In later years Phi Gamma Chi assumed another vital role as keeper of the tradition by maintaining an examination file for those professors who gave the same tests each year.

The campus yearbook also developed fitfully into a Polish-American publication during the interwar years. Issued irregularly under various titles, it was usually a simple memoir of the graduating classes. Occasionally it went beyond that: the 1928 volume, mainly in English, commemorated the twenty-fifth anniversary of Dąbrowski's death, and a stylish literary work in English was directed by Father Edward Skrocki in 1934. In 1938, it appeared for the first time as the *Eagle*.

When the Seminary moved to Orchard Lake, the local press described the school as "the only one, perhaps in which piety and orderly observance of religious duties are combined with an almost idolatrous worship of the great American game of baseball."[4] It seems fitting that the momentous news of the purchase of the Academy property should reach the students during an away baseball game. The beginnings of the athletic program at the Seminary are shrouded in vague records, but an athletic field on the old campus and nearby sandlots in Detroit provided the first playing fields by the turn of the century. Seminary sports served obvious purposes—recreational, "character" building, communal identity, institutional public relations. In the 1920s and 1930s, the heyday of varsity sports, athletic programs introduced future priests to the kind of work they might be expected to do with the youth in Polish-American parishes. Attendance was mandatory for all students, even at so-called recreational games.

To judge by the earliest accounts and the proudly worn PS emblem, Seminary sports at the start were an early form of Polish Catholic action. A bruising football game with Detroit College (the University of Detroit) in the 1890s inaugurated intercollegiate athletic competition at the Seminary and helped to create the American myth of Polish physical strength and dogged determination. Early college football was a rough and informal game; and the Seminary team was forced to disband because, as the local tradition has it, its intimidating field behavior made it difficult to recruit opponents. Football was revived at the Lake in 1912-1914, only to be dropped, in part because church officials objected to the participation of priesthood candidates, especially of theologians. Varsity baseball had better luck. The early Seminary teams, perceived and known as "Giants," were competing with other colleges by 1900. They enjoyed excellent records after leaving Detroit, but the sport was abandoned after the 1932 season because of financial constraints imposed by the Great Depression.

Basketball, in 1913 the last of the major sports to be introduced, had the most remarkable history. Moderately successful in its first decade, the triumphant seasons of 1923-1933 under coach Father Leo Malinowski provided St. Mary's—the team name that replaced Polish Seminary—with its legendary sports history. The 1924-1925 varsity team in particular, boasting "Michigan's Greatest Five" (Stan Stungis, Andy Bocianski, John Glaudel, Jerry Juchniewicz, and Andy Wotta), were the stuff out of which American Catholic schools have been built. It is hard to explain the ability of St. Mary's to compete against larger and better financed schools in those years. Possibly other colleges had yet to recuit the best talent in the still segregated Polish communities. The opportunity for players to work together for as many as eleven years from high school through theology also contributed to their success as a team.

The High School also introduced basketball in 1913 and matched the success of the College-Seminary team under

Father Malinowski in 1925-1927 and under Father Wotta, who returned to his Alma Mater, in 1927-1934. In 1933, the High School captured the state Class C championship. High School baseball was consistently if not as famously successful as basketball from 1913 to 1932, when it was abandoned for four years. Football, however, never took hold in the High School in this period. Teams were fielded only in 1913-1915 and 1930-1932.

The existence of the College Department after 1927 and the formation of the Michigan-Ontario Collegiate Conference (MOCC) with St. Mary's as a charter member in 1930 stimulated the expansion of the sports program. Varsity football was restored in 1930 (along with the debut of the school song, "Men of St. Mary's," by Rev. Theodore Kowalewski, at the first game). Except for a conference championship in 1932, the team suffered a string of dismal seasons. Perhaps they had lost what their early opponents had believed to be their secret weapon: the ability to conceal their plays by communicating in Polish. Finally, the drain on manpower at the start of the Second World War persuaded the school to abandon varsity competition. The College basketball teams won their conference championship three years running in 1930-1933. Track and field, golf, and tennis had short but successful runs in the College from the mid-thirties to the early forties before the war also brought them to a close.

A subsistence campus economy enabled the schools to carry on in spite of a low tuition which never covered more than half the cost of education and probably much less if one considers unpaid tuition and other forms of subsidy like the contributed services of priest-faculty. Students provided occasional labor on the farm in harvest time, in the kitchen, as librarians until 1932 and infirmarians from 1919 to 1925, in the printery, and as assistants to faculty administrators, the librarian and infirmarian. Working for a faculty member as a clerk or in a major student organization was especially important for it often initiated the training and recruitment of men who returned to staff Orchard Lake after ordination.

Many of the full-time workers in maintenance, the kitchen, or laundry were immigrants who worked at the Lake before going on to better paying jobs. Some, however, stayed long enough to emerge from anonymity: Clemens "Klimek" Zmysłowski in general maintenance from World War I until he died in 1969; Ignatius Barski who, as engineer, planned all maintenance work from 1916 to 1940; John Zasucha, a boiler operator for 43 years; Andrzej Żychowicz and "Stryja" (Uncle) Ciechoradzki in the laundry from the 1930s to the 1950s; and Sam Pastuch on the farm until it closed in Msgr. Szumal's administration.

In September, 1935, a corps of six Felician Sisters settled at Orchard Lake where they took over supervision of the chapels and domestic duties on campus. A special dispensation from a general chapter in 1959 allowed them to continue (still, in 1985) as the only ones of their congregation in such seminary work. They quickly became part of the fabric of the campus: Sister Luchesia, the first and chief telephone operator from 1935 to the mid-sixties; Sisters Aniela and Dorothy in the kitchens, laundry, and chapels; and others who served for shorter periods of time. They occupied the former faculty residence and fraternity house facing Orchard Lake until the construction of a convent over the new dining hall in 1966.

The produce of the farm, all kinds of donated services, the low wages and more than full work loads of the faculty and staff, the contributions of the Felicians, and the volunteer work of students accounted for a large part of the School's hidden income. Still, the labors of this scholastic village were not enough. The move to Orchard Lake and the expansion of facilities created a burdensome debt and increased the cost of maintenance. Unwillingness to turn away qualified seminarians who could not pay their way was consistent with the mission and values of Orchard Lake but exacted a substantial price in the long run. The general economic crisis of the 1930s aggravated the problem even as it curtailed the enrollment which would have brought relief.

The Seminary had long appealed for funds, but throughout the 1920s and 1930s, it steadily and systematically widened its base of support in the Polish-American community.

After a generation, as the first alumni convention pointed out in 1923, Polonia's commitment to the "Seminary" rested upon a tradition of preparation for secular professions as well as for the priesthood. During their first thirty-five years, the Seminary and the High School had educated more than 2,000 men, many of them ordained priests, but mostly others who had begun to make their mark in business, the professions, and other secular callings. Two of the first support organizations to emerge in the interwar years were built on the sense of obligation and loyalty among students, both past and present. The earlier of them was the Metropolitan Club—Scranton's was the first in 1919—begun as a campus organization but continued as a fraternal, social, and fund raising association in areas where alumni were numerous —Detroit, Chicago, Cleveland, New England, New Jersey, upstate New York, New York City, northern Pennsylvania, Pittsburgh, and Toledo. Many of the clubs, however, depended on the motivation and interest of a core group, formed during the student years, which often waned with time and distance.

An alumni association with regional units, something directed centrally from the campus, offered hope for more consistent support. Orchard Lake's expansive definition of alumni—all who attended as well as graduated from the schools—opened the door to broad community involvement. During the immigrant era the two alumni conventions were really short-lived priests' gatherings significant in the clerical politics of Polonia, as well as Seminary support organizations. The third alumni convention in 1916 prefigured the transition to the more American pattern during Father Grupa's administration. Father Anthony Kłowo was directly responsible for the change in 1923 by gathering 400 alumni, both lay and clerical, at Orchard Lake for their organizing convention. They were grouped into districts in the same year, and a section of *Sodalis* was reserved for reaching each of them directly until the publication of *Orchard Lake Alumnus* began in 1937. Their fund raising activities for Orchard Lake were expanded in 1930 when the Detroit District initiated widely imitated local banquets and friendship parties. In 1935, Rev. John Mioduszewski defined their spirit in the "Hymn of the Alumni of the Polish Seminary": "Hej Koledzy, hej Alumni z Seminarjum Polskiego!/Bądźmy wszyscy z tego dumni, ześmy z Rodu Laszego!"[5]

Women, of course, had long played a significant but well-defined role in Polonia in their own religious congregations, cultural and devotional associations, and insurance fraternals, as well as in separate departments in the Polish National Alliance and the Polish Roman Catholic Union of America. Despite feminist overtones in the behavior of some women and their organizations, the community perceived them primarily as channels for the maintenance of national and ethnic identity, especially through the family. The cult of Mary reflected their role in the formation of priests, though they had little to do formally with the Seminary until the 1930s. Bishop Stephen Woźnicki, the first bishop alumnus of the Seminary, collaborated with Msgr. Krzyżosiak and Chester Kozdrój, Detroit Alumni District President, to crystalize their potential into the Ladies Auxiliary of the Alumni Association. The first three chapters were based in the parishes of St. Florian's (Hamtramck), St. Hyacinth's on the east side, and St. Francis' on the west side of Detroit. Campus priests would drive them to and from the Lake to work at "unromantic and yet motherly chores"—ironing the seminarians' shirts and putting up the produce of the farm. As their number grew and they raised funds, they were able to provide "furniture, appliances and such things as more often than not demand a woman's taste and touch." Their prayers, "offered on their beads," and their influence in recruiting young men for the Seminary further sustained the values for which Orchard Lake stood.[6]

The Seminary also reached out formally to the parishes, many of whose priests had been trained there for two generations. In 1934, two campus priests were relieved of their teaching duties to alert Polonia to the Golden Jubilee of the schools. Their tour, which amounted to the first national fund raising campaign, took them to over 100 parishes in 77 cities in 11 dioceses. During the 1920s, Father Kłowo and others also renewed the formal relationship of the early years with the Polish Roman Catholic Union of America. A lodge had been organized on campus in 1914. In 1928, the Union's convention appropriated $4,000 for the support of the Seminary over the next three years. Then, as the Depression, declining enrollment and debt burdened the Seminary in the 1930s, the PRCUA and other fraternals like the Polish Union of the United States in Wilkes-Barre were invited to represent American Polonia in securing the Seminary's future. Initially, the PRCUA donated $1,000 on the occasion of the Seminary's Golden Jubilee in 1935, and over $23,000 additional from 1937 to 1941. These events were but prelude, however, to a more significant commitment.

The prospect in 1941 that the entire Archdiocese of Detroit might be forced into bankruptcy united all the support groups of the Seminary. During the building boom of the twenties, Catholic Detroit had borrowed far beyond its ability to repay principle in the lean thirties. When, at last, the Archdiocese was unable to guarantee interest payments, the banks threatened foreclosure. Clearly, though, churches, schools, rectories, and convents were not the kinds of things that permitted lenders to recoup more than a small fraction of their investment. However, the Archdiocese possessed some desirable properties that could be converted easily into cash. They included the Chancery Building on Washington Boulevard, Holy Sepulchre Cemetery, Sacred Heart Seminary, and the Orchard Lake campus. As a corporation sole, the Archbishop of Detroit owned all of them as well as nearly all the parish property in his jurisdiction. A threat to the corporation, no matter what the particular source of weakness, was a threat to each of the corporation's holdings. To meet the danger, Archbishop Edward Mooney decided to incorporate each institution separately—and speedily—to free them and the Archdiocese from the claims of creditors.

The legal status of the three schools was somewhat confusing by this time. The Seminary had been incorporated in 1917, but its corporate status had lapsed in 1934 for failing to file the required annual reports with the State of Michigan. Meanwhile, following the reorganization in 1927, the other two departments had been incorporated in 1929 as "St. Mary's Polish High School and College." On the surface their educational mission was the same as that of any other high school or college in Michigan except that it included the teaching of Polish. The members, officers, and trustees of the corporation were required to be practical Roman Catholics and graduates of one of the two schools. The Bishop and Chancellor of the Diocese of Detroit were members and officers of the corporation ex officio; the Diocese owned and operated the corporation.

Early in 1941, Archbishop Mooney initiated the restructuring of the Seminary and its allied schools through his auxiliary, Bishop Woźnicki. A hastily convened meeting of the corporation, really just five administrator-members from Orchard Lake, decided to amend the charter. The collective name was changed to "SS. Cyril and Methodius Seminary, St. Mary's College, St. Mary's High School" and the purpose of the Seminary, to provide "facilities for the training of priests as are prescribed by the Canon Law of the Church," was added formally to that of the High School and College. Ownership of the property on which the Schools functioned was transferred to the newly re-named corporation. All members and officers of the corporation still had to be practical Roman Catholics and with three exceptions alumni of one of the schools as well. The exceptions were the Archbishop of Detroit (the ex officio chairman) and the presidents of the Polish Roman Catholic Union and the Polish Union of the United States. The other members were five administrators (the Rector, Vice-Rector and Procurator of the Seminary, the Vice-President of the College, and the Principal of the High School), the President of the Alumni Association, nine alumni elected by the Board of the Association, and the presidents of the local districts of the Association.

The evening of the decision to amend the charter, Rector Krzyżosiak prevailed on the State Superintendent of Education to call a special meeting of the State Board of Education for the next morning to approve the proposed changes. The Board approved the new educational corporation promptly, and the Rector filed the new papers of incorporation with the State Commission, which granted a new charter on February 24, 1941. Incorporation lifted the immediate threat from the creditors of the Archdiocese. Revision of the by-laws in the year that followed fleshed out the principles, implied as well as explicit, in the new charter. The Alumni were particularly important in a process that was aided by Bishop Woźnicki, Archbishop Mooney, Federal Judge and Alumni Association President Arthur Kościnski, Judge Frank Schemanske of the Detroit Recorder's Court, and Assistant Corporation Counsel Walter Vashak (Washak) of the City of Detroit.

The sole administrative function of the corporation was to select from its number a fifteen-member Board of Trustees composed of a majority of Roman Catholic clergy. The Archbishop of Detroit was ex officio chairman and the National President of the Alumni ex officio Vice-Chairman of the Board. Archbishop Mooney was an active chairman, attending most meetings and taking part in major decisions on finance, appointments, and admissions policy, not to mention reincorporation. Occasionally, however, the President of the Alumni Association, a layman, chaired board meetings, a practice which became normal under Mooney's successor, Archbishop John Dearden. It was, to say the least, unusual for a layman to preside, in fact, over the governing board of a Roman Catholic Seminary, one of the many parts of an unwritten compromise in which Polish-American Catholics were allowed considerable autonomy in the management of their church affairs.

The new arrangement was welded together financially with the aid of the Polish Roman Catholic Union. At the time that the charter was revised, the PRCU assumed a mortgage on the property of the schools. Annual donations ranging from $6,500 to $9,071 by the Union during the next five years eased the initial burden of repayment, scheduled to be completed by 1956. The alumni convention of 1942 brought the reorganization publicly to a conclusion, and the corporation began to function as a trust of the American Polonia.

Externally a response to a financial and administrative

crisis, the events of 1941-1942 spoke also to Orchard Lake's growing sense of what it was about. Self-definition was aided somewhat by the prejudice of native, white, Anglo-Saxon Americans, apparent even in the rural Michigan environment in which the Seminary found itself after 1909. More critically, Orchard Lake was challenged to justify itself within the Church by the American Catholic hierarchy, many of Irish and some of German origin. In the heated, super-patriotic atmosphere of the First World War and the 1920s, the hope of many bishops that ethnic identities would disappear into a common American nationality seemed almost in view. Faith in the American melting pot caused numerous slights, real and imagined, from the American hierarchy toward the recent immigrants who, together with their children, numbered over half the American Catholic population.

The new Code of Canon Law which went into effect in 1917 only added to the pressure to Americanize. In the minds of many church officials it appeared to doom national or ethnic parishes by affirming the territorial nature of the Catholic parish for the future. Diocesan superintendents of schools in Buffalo and Brooklyn further insisted in 1923 that schools instruct only in English as required by state law (and in Buffalo at least) brought down the wrath of Polonia upon the ordinary. The frigid relationship between Archbishop Mundelein and the Polish clergy of Chicago, rooted in very different notions of the social basis of the American Catholic Church, was well known. Pittsburgh's bishop, meanwhile, found it difficult to raise money for a diocesan school building program among Poles and other recent immigrants who did not believe it would support their community structure and ethnic heritage.

Bishops who hoped to accelerate the assimilation they deemed inevitable withdrew seminarians of Polish background from SS. Cyril and Methodius Seminary in order to place them in their own diocesan or provincial seminaries where Polish language and culture were not always emphasized. The opening of major new seminaries for Chicago and Philadelphia and declining enrollment from Buffalo and Pittsburgh removed Orchard Lake from as much as half its normal pool of seminary recruits in the 1920s. The theologate quickly lost about half its enrollment, and its very existence as a national institution was brought into question.

Bishop Michael Gallagher of Detroit found himself under additional pressure from fellow bishops who wanted to close the Seminary on the grounds that it had no basis in church law. No generalization based on national origin really holds for all, however. Bishop Gallagher, though of Irish descent, continued to send Polish-Americans who aspired to the priesthood to Orchard Lake, founded some twelve additional Polish (only formally territorial) parishes in his diocese, and personally searched in Rome for the petition of Father Moczygemba by which Leo XIII had authorized the foundation of the Seminary. (The document turned up serendipitously at Orchard Lake itself in 1938.)

Ever since the 1870s, Polish immigrants and their children had tried to explain themselves as they carved out a living in America. The Polish Seminary, through its priest-educators and students, had been at the heart of that self-examination and preparation for life. As the High School and College were opened to boys of Polish parentage without ambitions for the Catholic priesthood but who wished to maintain their Polish tradition and culture, the faculty and administration at Orchard Lake came to a clearer understanding of their social mission. Polishness was to be preserved at the Lake "not as an entirely exotic phenomenon in American life but as a means whereby American culture and the Polish heritage may be merged, so that in the lives of the Polish immigrant and his descendants each of these cultures may supplement each other." Ultimately, they believed that a living Polish culture would be "an effective method of safeguarding the Catholic faith of the Polish people . . . and that the religious faith and the love of Polish culture are intimately associated in the minds and hearts not only of the immigrants themselves but also of the second and third generations of their descendants."⁷ Neither Polish nor American, neither traditional nor modern, neither segregated from nor integrated with American society, they were Polish-American Catholic.

Aerial views of the Orchard Lake Campus as it appeared in the late 1920s and 1930s. Above: Looking out over the lake with the farm in the foreground. Below: From over the lake with the farm at the top.

The Faculty of 1927-1928. Seated, first row, left to right: Rev. Joseph Rybiński, Rev. Anthony Kłowo, Prof. Romuald Piątkowski, Rt. Rev. Msgr. Michael J. Grupa (Rector from 1917 to 1932), Prof. Ignacy Machnikowski, Rev. Francis Węgier, Rev. Constantine Cyran. Standing, second row, left to right: Rev. Boleslaus Milinkiewicz, Rev. Stanislaus Janicki, Rev. Michael Wojtusiak, Prof. Peter Łobaza, Prof. Andrew Martusiewicz, Rev. Andrew Wotta, Rev. Leo Malinowski, Rev. Stanislaus Grabowski. Standing in the rear, left to right: Rev. Alexander Cendrowski, Rev. Edward Krawczyk, Rev. Ladislaus Krzyżosiak, Rev. Ladislaus Krych, Rev. Francis X. Orlik, Rev. Theodore Kowalewski, Rev. Stanislaus Tenerowicz, Rev. Anthony Maksimik.

Left: Rt. Rev. Msgr. Anthony Kłowo (Rector from 1932 to 1937) flanked by Most Rev. Michael J. Gallagher, Bishop of Detroit, to the left and Most Rev. Joseph Plagens, Auxiliary Bishop of Detroit, to the right.

Below, left to right: Rt. Rev. Msgr. Edward Szumal (Rector from 1943 to 1956), Most Rev. Edward Mooney (Archbishop of Detroit), Rt. Rev. Msgr. Adalbert Żądala, and Rt. Rev. Msgr. Ladislaus Krzyżosiak (Rector from 1937 to 1943), attending a joint Preparatory-College commencement in the 1940s.

Above: View of the campus about 1920 from the junction of Commerce Road and Indian Trail. *Below:* The Seminary Building about 1920.

Above: The "Castle," the residence of the rector and priest professors, about 1920. Below: Residence of lay professors about 1920 (the "Frat House" in the early 1930s, the sisters convent from 1935 to 1966, and the laywomen's residence since 1966).

Above: Interior of the Gymnasium, the first dormitory for classics students in 1909, about 1920. Below: Exterior of the Gymnasium, the powerhouse to the left, about 1920.

Above: The refectory and classics dormitory about 1920. Below: The "Barracks," dormitory for older classics students, about 1920, prior to their reconstruction in 1927-1928.

Above: The Classics Chapel about 1920. Below: Interior of the Classics Chapel about 1920.

Above: The Refectory prior to its transformation into the Chapel after the fire of 1917. Below: The Classroom Building about 1920.

Above: The Physics Lecture Room about 1920. Below: Professor Peter Łobaza with his first-year Classics students in 1916.

Recreation at the Polish Seminary. Above: In 1913. Below: About 1916.

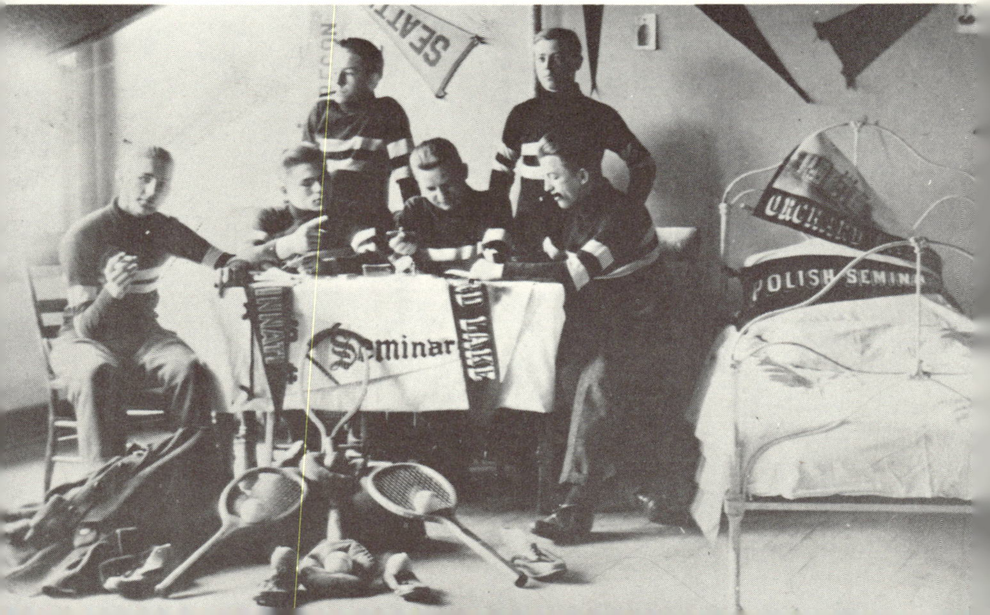

Above: The Seminary Football Team in 1913. Below: The College (Varsity) Basketball Team of 1920-1921.

Above: The College Basketball Team of 1924-1925, including "Michigan's Greatest Five." Below: Michigan High School Class C State Champions, 1933, with Coach Rev. Andrew C. Wotta.

IV. *The Ethnic Promise Fulfilled, 1942-1965*

POLISH-Americans learned who they were between the World Wars. Their children, born or reared in America, were their teachers. As Professor Francis Świetlik told an international conference of the emigration leadership in Warsaw in 1935: "Polonia in America is neither a Polish colony nor a national minority, but a component part of the great American nation, proud, however, of its Polish origin and careful to implant in the hearts of the younger generation a love for all that is Polish."[1] Some leaders of American Polonia were able to ignore Świetlik's description of their ethnic group as a basis for action. The educators and parents of the young did not have that luxury. The Polish-Americanization of the three schools at Orchard Lake, capped by their reincorporation of 1941, was the foundation for a program which sustained them through a changing world until the 1960s.

Polish-Americans, traditionally a self-effacing and self-sufficing ethnic group, found a providential mission for their seminary in the 1940s, nothing less than a role in the restructuring of American life on Christian principles through universalizing the Polish-American Catholic experience. This extraordinary identification with America was the life work of Father Valerius Jasiński. It was rooted in a view which had wide currency among European Catholic social thinkers in the early twentieth century and anticipated some widely held notions among Americans after 1945.

According to Jasiński, the United States was engaged in the early 1940s in a great struggle for liberty against Bolshevism and Hitlerism, its third such contest since the achievement of independence from England in the eighteenth century and the end of slavery in the nineteenth century. In his view, not yet widely shared outside Catholic circles, Bolshevism and Hitlerism were rooted in the destructive liberty unleashed by "Individualism, Protestantism, and Liberalism." Those three forces, responsible for forcing Catholic immigrants into ghetto-like separatism or slavish imitation of WASP American culture, were a plausible explanation for nativism in America since the 1830s. Cultural nativism was, Jasiński argued, unrealistic for it ignored the nature of man:

> a living insoluble organism whose blood, much less his psychic structure cannot be dissolved with impunity, that is, without destroying the entire man and annihilating in him whatever is good and wholesome . . . for the man who would ignore the cultural heritage of his forefathers would be as foolish as a horticulturist who should prefer untilled ground to a soil intelligently cultivated by his predecessor. Besides, a man who sets no store by the venerable endowment bequeathed to him by his ancestors—a culture that rose out of centuries of cooperation with divine grace—will learn to disregard every authority, whether of parents, superiors, the State, his God, and the church; he will become shallow, thoughtless, with no more ballast than a piece of cork on the billows. Such a man does not and cannot make a useful American citizen. We wonder if that false approach to solving America's assimilation problem has not decidedly intensified the nature of her plight in the war against Liberalism. In as much, then, as a faulty attempt at the problem heightens the moral crisis, a real solution can hasten America's victory in her third struggle for liberty.[2]

Father Jasiński's thinking was very much in the spirit of the age, at least among Catholics. The career of the distinguished College alumnus, Walter Ciszek, was living proof of its power. Born in Shenandoah, Pennsylvania, Ciszek joined the Jesuits in New York after taking the philosophy program at Orchard Lake. Stationed in eastern Poland at the outbreak of war in 1939, he continued to minister to Poles in the Russian zone of occupation. Soon swallowed up by Soviet prisons and camps, he eventually won a quasi-freedom, his existence officially ignored but serving all the while as an underground priest. His release in 1963 in exchange for a Soviet spy held in the United States coincided with the beginning of a shift in attitude toward the verities of the Cold War just as his imprisonment had heralded the ideological struggle between East and West.

Monsignor Edward Szumal, the sixth rector of the Polish Seminary, could only have guessed at the fate of Father Ciszek. Nevertheless, his message to the graduates of 1946 caught the mood of the times with a gloomy assessment of the state of America in which Orchard Lake's Catholic education was a sign of hope:

> The world sorely needs men whose thinking is clear and whose *courage* is high. Blessed by the precious heritage of Catholic Philosophy, you have at hand the means to satisfy these needs.
> You are witnesses to a sad spectacle: Strong, robust America unable to come to the relief of a sick world, because her minds cannot think; courageous, brave America yielding to temptation of appeasement and outright compromise with unethical principles; ideal-loving, God-fearing America espousing and promoting causes which are diametrically opposed to everything for what She had once stood. Its system of education based on questionable and false principles has weakened and is slowly nullyfying her "leavening" abilities over evil.
> We have won the war, but are losing the peace. Be ever mindful that you have the equipment which makes men just, noble and holy, and which makes nations great. Standing for and using these means will assure success in your work and will hasten the reign of justice and charity in the world at large.[3]

Father Jasiński lodged the problems of America and the hope for the future in ethnic and cultural issues. Their resolution was the starting point for moral renewal and salvation.

Not only was conformity to an Anglo or American ideal unrealistic, according to Jasiński, it deprived America of a powerful moral force in the contemporary struggle for liberty. The approach of the Catholic Church as teacher to all nations offered a realistic alternative by harnessing the powerful force of heritage to general social goals. Emphasizing "the necessity of correlating all effort with native endowment—language, culture, and custom . . . the Church accepts whatever is worthwhile and good . . . in any nationality, ennobles that, sanctifies it, and builds it organically into the Mystical Body of Christ."[4] In his theory of cultural pluralism, a reality with which Poles in America had wrestled at least since Dąbrowski's time, Jasiński concluded that each national group must "overcome its characteristic faults, at the same time cultivating its highest moral, spiritual, and intellectual qualities with which it can enrich the life of its adopted land."[5]

The historian Father Joseph Swastek, Jasiński's younger contemporary, was less hopeful for the survival of Polish culture in America. For an American-born historian (not a Polish moralist like Jasiński), that would not be surprising. Yet his response to the question, "What is a Polish American?" in 1944 was broadly similar to Jasiński's ideologically inspired analysis. His Polonia was "a complex organism composed of Polish and American elements—a compound in the main of Polish, Catholic institutions, traditions, and values, and of American urban, industrial, democratic, equalitarian conditions."[6] Though the Polish American submitted finally "to the influence of American conditions, the native American Pole did not in most instances break completely with his Polish heritage, displaying in this respect the characteristic individualism of his forebears. He retained the essential religious idealism of his parents by maintaining his adherence to Catholicism, strengthening sentiment with knowledge and understanding." If the Polish American differed from assimilated Americans, "it was only in the specific character of his heritage and perhaps in his larger possession of it."[7] Swastek's research into the early history of the Polish

Seminary and the Detroit parish in which it was founded, his editorship from 1948 to 1970 of *Polish American Studies,* the journal of the Polish American Historical Association which established its headquarters at Orchard Lake in 1949, and his classroom teaching and student symposia elaborated that message to a Polish ethnic audience and two generations of college students. Jasiński did much the same through the Seminary for over thirty years.

The Polish-American constituency from which Orchard Lake drew its life blood was dominated, as Swastek noted, by native-born children of immigrants. The shape of the third generation, the grandchildren of the immigrants, was hard to discern in 1944, though he lived long enough to see it and deal with it. World War II did more than pose a challenge from Hitlerism and Bolshevism. It also finally ended the Great Depression which had threatened the very existence of the Seminary. It brought prosperity and, through the new industrial unions, power as well to the working class constituencies which Orchard Lake graduates served. Maker of war material, supplier to burgeoning consumer demand after 1945, possessed of new economic and political power, Detroit Polonia never seemed stronger than it did during the 1940s. Prosperity financed and accelerated the movement of younger Poles on the east side of Detroit across Six Mile Road and then Eight Mile Road into the suburban communities of Macomb County. On the west side of the city they moved in the direction of and beyond Dearborn.

In the new suburbs the parishes were territorial (sometimes only in name); the array of ethnic institutions was largely missing; and the Polish language, even in its Americanized version, was heard less often. Life was still working class in character; and many of the old values survived, but assimilation made them externally indistinguishable from non-Polish parishes. The Polish parish network still offered opportunities, but they were of a different kind or made different demands on priests. From being one of the ethnic groups least likely to send its children to high school and college, Poles equalled (during the Cold War) and exceeded (during the Vietnam War) national norms for higher education among all Catholic groups except the Irish.

New Polish immigrants, settling in significant number in the Detroit area after 1948, were frequent exceptions to the rules governing the development of the older immigration and its children. They of course had a more vivid memory of Poland than the aging members of the great migration early in the century. Independent Poland between the wars or People's Poland after 1948 shaped their national identities, not the ill-defined cultural Polishness of the partition period. They tended to be better educated, spoke contemporary Polish, and were more urban in background. Politics, be it the refusal of veterans to return to the communist-dominated nation after 1945 or rejection of the post-war system by others, was a more important factor in their decision to emigrate. While they often joined forces with the older Polonia, they also expressed themselves between 1948 and 1980 in new veterans' groups, Polish supplementary schools, and the Mission Church of the Society of Christ in Sterling Heights. The new Polonia, especially its children, also advanced more promptly into the mainstream of American middle class life.

The neighborhoods which Poles of the great migration had settled in the 19th century were now resettled by new immigrants, mainly blacks from the rural American South where a feudal agricultural system was breaking up. The impulse for the new migration came from a variety of political and economic forces—labor markets transformed and expanded in the North by military purchases, federal subsidies to large land owners and agricultural mechanization in the South which eliminated small farms and farm work, and housing renewal and freeway construction in northern cities in the 1950s and 1960s. Altogether, they transformed the face of the old Polish neighborhoods, while subsidized mortgages and veterans benefits opened up new opportunities for the children and grandchildren of the aging immigrants.

The relationship between this native American Polonia and Poland was ambiguous. It combined sentimental attachment and growing distance. As Swastek pointed out:

"Toward the Polish language his [the Polish-American's] feelings were mixed, varying from complete neglect to intelligent, loving cultivation. Similarly conflicting were his attitudes towards Poland; for the old idealistic concept he substituted a more realistic view involving different degrees of interest in Poland's cultural achievements and at most some sentimental solicitude for its political vissicitudes."[8] Rev. Edward Szumal, rector from 1943 to 1956, is remembered for the "loving cultivation" of Polish language and culture. Though all rectors have been fluent in Polish, Father Szumal's frequent visits to the land of his fathers as a student in the 1920s marked him exceptionally as one of those who came to Polish culture through the immigrant experience.

The European War, which became a World War in 1941 with the participation of the Soviet Union, Japan, and the United States, touched Orchard Lake poignantly in every aspect of its identity. The war had begun in 1939 with the calamitous defeat and division of Poland by Germany and the Soviet Union. Soon afterwards, the first of the many priests who transformed the Seminary residence into a Polish refugee center arrived on campus. In 1941, Father Anthony Maksimik organized Faculty War Relief for Poland. Monthly, for three years, members of the faculty contributed money to purchase supplies at cost from local wholesalers and merchants. Seminarians, supervised by Father Maksimik, packed shipments of about 100 boxes each month to different destinations. Father Maksimik himself paid for the shipments. Others, Fathers Cyran, Wotta, and Rybiński, and Professor Łobaza, continued the work independently when the original program was merged into larger Polish-American efforts.

A steady stream of individuals, forced to relocate by the war, passed through Orchard Lake during the war under various sponsors. The best known of them were 31 young Polish boys who arrived from camps in India in the fall of 1945. Accepted at first at the request of the American Bishops War Relief Committee, they were guaranteed full maintenance and education by the Schools. The fund drives to assist them that were launched by Rector Szumal and Fathers Edward Popielarz and Alexander Cendrowski in December 1945 laid the foundations for the Friends of the Orchard Lake Schools, a permanent major appeal to Polonia parishes. The "Chłopcy z Polski," (Boys from Poland) as they were known, were remarkably career-oriented; many of them became priests and other professionals. When they evolved into the Knights of Dąbrowski, they held regular reunions at the Lake and contributed materially to the schools. Led by Dr. Edward Wajda, the Knights ultimately served as Orchard Lake's most effective publicists in the Chicago area.

The "Chłopcy" were also a reminder of the major outcomes of the war—the occupation of Poland by the Soviet Union in 1944-45, and the establishment of a communist regime by 1948, which discouraged many of the war's refugees from returning home. As a major Cold War event, the sovietization of Poland put Polish-Americans squarely behind the crusade to define and defend American values and interests against communism and Russian imperial expansion. It also cut off American Polonia from normal contact with contemporary Polish culture and economic development. If, as Father Jasiński hoped, America or the American Church were to be imbued "with the beautiful and rich worth of the thousand-years-old Polish culture," that realm of "service to Christian civilization written in indelible characters," it would have to be from "the bedrock of Christian civilization which they [Poles in America] inherited from their forebears . . ."[9]

As Orchard Lake reminded itself of its Polish links in the 1940s and lost contact with the mainstream of development in the "old country," it also defined itself more sharply and in new ways as Catholic. Building on that "bedrock of Christian civilization" American Poles could rest assured that "their work here has always been constructive." The Seminary continued that work by reemphasizing its homiletic approach to doctrine, current issues, and the re-Christianization of America. In 1941, it convened the first Polish Homiletic Congress in America, which as an informal association of priests also served to unify the Polish-American clergy. Meanwhile, the Seminary proclaimed its teaching mission more quietly but just as clearly by building the Kłowo Homiletic Collection of print materials into a major library holding.

The Seminary's renowned Schola Cantorum, founded in 1938, carried a similar message to a mass audience. Under the direction of Rev. Henry Waraksa, the Schola reached national and international audiences through annual Christmas broadcasts, recordings of Polish Christmas carols, Marian and Lenten music, television appearances, and major concerts in Detroit's Orchestra Hall. Together with the Prep Glee Club, which Father Waraksa founded, the College Choir, and the Campus Orchestra, the Schola established a popular image of Orchard Lake as Catholic and Polish that lasted long after its own glory days.

At the urging of Cardinal Mooney, an active chairman of the Board of Trustees, the College began in the 1940s to admit only men who intended to study for the priesthood. As Orchard Lake turned its back on the lay college for which Father Joseph Gierut, the Dean of the College, had sought accreditation, the Archdiocese of Detroit gradually incorporated the College into its general plan for seminary education. During Bishop Gallagher's time, divinity students from the Michigan province at St. Mary's were allowed, if they wished, to complete their theological studies at SS. Cyril and Methodius. From 1940, however, they and the graduates of Sacred Heart, the diocesan seminary college in Detroit, were required to attend St. Mary's Seminary in Cincinnati. Meanwhile, Detroit laid plans to enter the ranks of the other great metropolitan sees by establishing its own school of theology. When Mooney finally opened St. John's in Plymouth in 1949, he required all Michigan candidates for the priesthood to attend. Men of Polish background who were interested in working in Polish parishes were allowed to do their college work at Orchard Lake, even if they were graduates of Sacred Heart's high school, before going on to St. John's. Together with divinity students from other dioceses in the Northeast and Midwest, they assured the College a stable annual enrollment of about 90-110 through the 1960s. Concurrently, the faculty at each of the Orchard Lake Schools became exclusively clerical as the old Polish lay instructors died or retired.

The High School was affected by campus-wide trends since it regularly sent a number of students on to the College and Seminary and shared faculty and administrators with the other two schools. Known increasingly from 1942 as the Preparatory School, it drew students largely from the Polish parish schools of urban Detroit and by way of long-established contacts with alumni priests in the Midwest and Northeast. The World War saved the Preparatory from near extinction. Reeling under the impact of the "Roosevelt Recession" of the late thirties, enrollment fell to a low of 49 students in 1941, when the possibility of exemption from Selective Service for high school seniors intending to follow a divinity program encouraged new applicants. The Seminary connection benefited each school in like manner in this and later wars.

In the "new" College Seminary, a major athletic program was less relevant to student and institutional goals. As the North Central visitation team put it in 1941: "If there is one thing certain about St. Mary's College, it is that the athletic program is not running away with the institution."[10] Moreover, the muscular Christianity of the interwar period —a kind of American Catholic action—gave way to a formation style emphasizing the growth of militant, articulate, and rigorous intellectuality. Varsity college football was abandoned in 1942 after a string of disappointing seasons. Basketball continued until 1949, after which the athletic program became an entirely intramural affair for the next twenty-five years.

The High School followed a somewhat different road. Football was restored in 1944, as baseball had been in 1936, though without much team success until 1955. Track and field were introduced in 1947, and an outdoor oval track was constructed in 1959. Indoor track was dropped in 1956, and the indoor track in the Gymnasium sacrificed to construct a small stage. The result was that the High School established a strong image in Southeastern Michigan through its athletic program. The program was also inspiration for founding the Moms and Dads Club. Organized in 1952 to manage High School games, the club became a significant fundraiser for renovation, maintenance, and equipment purchase.

The most vivid expression of Orchard Lake's Catholic and Polish-American character was the erection of the Marian Shrine during Msgr. Filipowicz's rectorship. Construction began in August 1961. Representative of the material progress, ideology, and ambition of Polish-Americans, the Shrine was planned as the focus of the new campus of the 1960s on the site of the old farm and was inspired by two visions of Mary—America's Immaculate Conception and Poland's Our Lady of Częstochowa. Perhaps unintentionally, it was also a midwestern counterpart to the Polish Shrine of American Częstochowa in Doylestown, Pennsylvania, and the Polish chapel in the Cathedral of the Immaculate Conception in Washington.

The design of alumnus Walter Różycki of Detroit, embracing the principles of architectural modernism, anticipated the liturgical changes which swept the American Church in the 1960s and broke down many of the formal distinctions between clergy and laity in favor of a community of worship. The construction exhibited a preference for natural, exposed materials—flagstone, mahogany, Douglas fir, and roughly cut marble. The stained glass windows, which took up most of the wall space, and the unobstructed interior linked the interior to its external setting. Dominated inside and out by the opposed reverse quadrants of the roof, the Shrine Chapel suggested the haven of a protective avenue of trees in a field-like setting. Mary, as another kind of haven, symbolically welcomed visitors at the entrance, guiding them without obstacle to her Son in the altar area, a more formally constructed area focusing on the sacrifice of Christ. Six private chapels off the sacristy in the rear were dedicated to Mary under different titles.

The Shrine's principle icon—an immense statue of Mary overhanging the main entrance—was based on a painting of Our Lady of Orchard Lake by another alumnus, Joseph

Jankowski of Cleveland. Jankowski's Mary was Slavic-American and youthful, a serious but not sorrowful image of elegant and elongated dimension, a straightforward contemporary idealization. It was translated and transformed into a monumental copper-sculptured shell weighing over a ton and a half by Clarence VanDusen of Cleveland. This more traditionally maternal and Slavic Mary was put in place on November 30, 1962. The dedication of the Chapel took place the following May with two alumni, Rev. Alexander Zaleski, auxiliary bishop of Detroit, representing Archbishop Dearden, as celebrant and Archbishop John Król of Philadelphia as homilist, leading the homage to Our Lady of Orchard Lake.

Throughout the forties, fifties, and sixties the curricula of the three schools remained static. Courses were highly structured with a predictable, fixed content as though they were the body of revealed truth. If anything, the emphasis on the preparation of priesthood candidates in the College narrowed the curricular focus by removing the need for any major but a B.A. in Philosophy. The Bachelors of Science and Philosophy were abandoned, as were courses in mathematics and all sciences but physics. Thirty-three or thirty-four college courses per year, no electives, and a schedule in which members of a class went through the cycle of courses together were the hallmarks of a standardized, efficient, easily administered curriculum.

The practice of sharing teachers and administrators by each of the three schools gave underlying consistency and coherence to the classroom experience on campus. Rigid to some and rigorous to others, the curriculum at its best served the mission of Orchard Lake and the cause of educational excellence. In Cold War America mission and excellence were taken for granted. According to Father Jasiński, the Polish Seminary offered a "thorough, comprehensive, Catholic education and training on a par with the best in European or American Seminaries."[11] Orchard Lake's commitment to cultural pluralism contributed to the major variation from the curricular standards of American Catholic education. It was the Seminary's proud boast that "classes are conducted in Latin, English, and Polish—which opens up for the students treasures of three very different but rich cultural traditions."[12]

Intellectual formation outside the classroom illuminated what went on inside. Student life still sustained the tradition of "imbuing the living organism of the country with the beautiful and rich worth of the thousand-year-old Polish culture"—that realm of "service to Christian civilization written in indelible characters." The Polish Literary Society, still active in play production, helped to create the first "Polish Room"—a gallery of photographs, memorabilia, and folk art dealing with Polish history and culture. And as Polish disappeared as a language of instruction in the High School, Fathers Francis Orlik and Edward Skrocki compensated for the decline in 1941 by expanding the English Oratorical Contest to include a Polish section.

Sodalis became a purely faculty publication in 1942, also reflecting the decline in student facility with Polish. Also befitting the post-immigrant era, students and faculty began to evaluate their own histories more critically. In the 1930s, St. Mary's was one of the few colleges in America where one could fulfill a major graduation requirement, the Senior Thesis, by studying one's ethnic past. Encouraged by Father Grupa and especially by young instructors like Bruno Stefan, Peter Ostafin, and Raymond Czarnik in the late 1930s, St. Mary's had to be the only college which recognized the Polish-American past as fit for study by undergraduates. In the hands of Father Swastek that interest blossomed in the 1940s. The Polish American Historical Association and *Polish American Studies,* the journal of the PAHA, both established themselves on the campus in 1949. As editor of the journal until 1970 and *de facto* executive secretary of the Association much of that time, Swastek successfully represented a subject which many believed or hoped would soon shrivel and die. With then Librarian Father Walter Ziemba he launched and later directed the college students in an annual Founder's Day symposium from 1952 to 1977. Using the occasion of Father Dąbrowski's name day, they reflected formally and publicly on Polish-American and

Polish history and culture. The results often found their way into the *Studies* and influenced the content of the campus yearbook.

The Thomistic philosophy which dominated Catholic higher education at mid-century found public expression in the annual St. Thomas Aquinas Day Programs. Directed by Father Jasiński and sponsored by the theologate, they were inaugurated in 1942, appropriately for an era concerned with mission, with the topic, "Does our Seminary have a reason for its existence?" Through the years they strove to "apply Thomistic principles to contemporary problems." The topic for 1945 amounted to a virtual summary of the curriculum and a challenge to society: "Democracy in the light of (1) Aristotle's and St. Thomas' teaching on Democracy, (2) The American Constitution, (3) The Polish Constitution, and (4) Pius XII's 1944 Christmas message." Father Jasiński also founded, in 1954, the SS. Cyril and Methodius Apostolate on Pope Pius XII's Roman notion of Christian ecumenism: "We desire nothing more ardently than that all who are known by the name of Christian should, under the patronage and following the example of St. Cyril, promote with everlasting zeal the happy return of our dissenting brethren in the East to us and to the one church of Jesus Christ."[13]

The spirit of intellectual rigor and achievement took new forms when Father Walter Ziemba was appointed College Dean of Studies in 1957. During his first year in office the Aquinas Academy, the Skarga Society, and the Conrad Club took root. The Academy, a lecture-discussion club, sought with a confidence that daunts a later generation "to discover the significance of the created world as it is reflected in literature, science, philosophy, and the arts."[14] Skarga was founded to develop public speaking abilities through practice, annual Christmas readings, debate, oratorical contests, and dramatic productions. Eventually, it assumed the mantle of the Polish Literary Society and Phi Gamma Chi as the principle play production group on campus and continued vigorously through the 1980s as a basic student support group for the Communication Arts department and a major social activity in the College. The Conrad Club encouraged creative writing, giving permanent form and personal expression to the reflection and persuasive technique promoted by the Academy and Skarga. Its members, "apostles of the written word," edited *Pen and Inklings* as well as *Surge,* the college literary magazine.

It is tempting to reflect on what the patrons chosen for the troika of 1957-1958 might say of what has been done in their names. Each of them represented a rigorous approach on behalf of a cause greater than himself: St. Thomas, reconciling reason and natural law with the faith and divine law of the medieval church; Piotr Skarga, the apocalyptic prophet of the Polish Catholic Reformation, demanding a return to a just and ordered society; Joseph Conrad, submitting his adult life to the discipline of art and the mastery of a foreign language. Symbols to a generation which valued order and ordered its values, they guided a new generation into another kind of era at the Lake.

The forties, fifties, and sixties were the golden age of the written word on campus. Two student publications from that time still flourish—the College's *Lake Oracle,* reestablished in 1944, and the High School's *Prep Laker,* begun in 1958. The campus yearbook, now known as the *Eagle,* emerged as the premier student activity at Orchard Lake. Its carefully constructed essays on the historical background, cultural premises, and devotional experiences of the Orchard Lake Schools frame an era as clearly they record the march of graduates through reminiscence and photograph.

Guided by the firm administrative hand of Rev. Wallace Filipowicz, rector from 1956 to 1967, the campus underwent the most dramatic physical changes in its history. Former students rose to the challenge of the era in 1956 by financing the construction of a new Alumni Memorial Library on Seminary Road. With the transfer of 25,000 volumes from the third floor of the Classroom building to the functional new library in September, 1957, the alumni might well have taken comfort in the physical consolidation of the gains made at the Lake. The Marian Shrine followed five years later; and as the larger than life Mary was being assembled for placement on the Shrine Chapel, ground was broken in 1962 for a separate residence for the College seminarians and a connected classroom building and indoor recreational lounge. A functional assemblage of boxy units, it was occupied by the College seminarians, then in the Ark. The Ark itself was gradually converted to offices for development and for the Orchard Lake Centers.

The steady pace of construction continued in 1966, when a new dining hall, sponsored by the Ladies Auxiliary, replaced the refectory in the renamed Activities Building. The second story above the new Dining Hall served as the second convent for the Felician Sisters while their former residence was converted to the use of laywomen workers. The Preparatory students remained in the Barracks until 1971, when a residence hall was constructed for them at a cost of nearly $2,000,000, half of it with a $1,000,000 loan from the Polish Roman Catholic Union. Finally, a fieldhouse named after its donor, Robert Dombrowski, was completed in 1973 at a cost of $800,000. Throughout the 1960s, the face of the new campus was gradually altered under the management of the Procurator-Treasurer, Rev. Stanley Milewski. The old farm buildings were demolished, and both the old and new campuses were integrated and made more usable. A roadway was cut through the center of campus in 1962. Landscaping, parking lots, and a carport provided significant amenities. The campus was tied into the Detroit Water System, and storm sewers leading into Orchard Lake provided essential drainage.

Except for the loan from the PRCU, the cost of the second building era, 4.85 million dollars, was drawn from annual surpluses. Only a fraction of the operating budgets and reserves were provided by ordinary fees and tuition. The bulk was derived from the contributions of American Polonia and particular constituencies of the Schools. The groundwork for systematic support had been laid in the 1920s and 1930s with the Alumni Association, the Ladies Auxiliary, the special relationship with the Polish Catholic fraternals, and the Golden Jubilee drive in the parishes.

Aided by their alumni, the Orchard Lake Schools significantly expanded their financial base in the 1940s and 1950s. Father Gierut's effort to have the College accredited stimulated the creation by him of the Dąbrowski Foundation in 1941 to provide the stable annual income that the North Central Association of Colleges and Secondary Schools expected of its members. On the initiative of Msgr. Francis Kasprowicz, president of the Trenton Alumni District, the Foundation was incorporated in 1943 to enroll members as annual contributors to academic improvement—library collection development, faculty publications, science laboratories, and general expenses. After 1945, an appeal on behalf of the "Chłopcy z Polski" was converted to an annual mail drive, the "Friends of the Orchard Lake Seminary," under the direction of Father Edward Popielarz. In 1952, Msgr. Casimir Piejda of Syracuse pioneered major growth in the Friends campaign by enrolling an entire parish. The names and addresses of parishioners were sent to Orchard Lake, which appealed directly to each of them with the support of the pastor. Through the good offices of John and Robert Slavsky in 1953, an advertising agency transformed the simple plea for help into a sophisticated, informational campaign. By 1960, 170 parishes had been enrolled; and the mechanization of mailing under Father Ziemba in 1957 permitted the dispatch of over a quarter of a million pieces of mail. Founder's Day, the largest and most sophisticated fund raising operation in the history of the Schools, evolved in the same period from modest beginnings. Using an idea which the Board of Directors of Guardian Angel Orphanage of the Felician Sisters had developed, the Detroit District of the Alumni Association organized the first of the annual parties at one hundred dollars per ticket in 1953. At its peak in the 1970s, Founder's Day seemed headed toward a million dollar one-day fund raising capacity, reaching beyond the traditional Orchard Lake constituency to non-alumni and non-Poles with the aid of that constituency.

The mechanics as well as the scope of fund raising improved significantly in the fifties, but they rested as they had in Father Dąbrowski's time on an unwritten contract between Polish Catholics and their priests. That relationship had solidified after 1915 as turmoil in the immigrant Polish-American parish subsided, and the clergy demonstrated their loyalty to the Polish identity within the American church. In its expanded version of the parochial collection, Orchard Lake fulfilled the implied contract by training and forming priesthood candidates for service in Polish parishes at far below the real cost; meanwhile, Polonia collectively provided the remainder in order to sustain its values. Orchard Lake's priests and students prayed—the mass especially—and Polonia was a loyal congregation.

Singularly loyal members of the community—human symbols of the contract between Polonia and the Seminary—were singled out for recognition. In 1949, the Board of Trustees awarded the first Fidelitas Medal "to an outstanding American Catholic of Polish descent for fidelity in serving God and Country through the realization of the religious and cultural ideas of our forefathers." The first recipient was Msgr. Lucyan Bójnowski, the "immigrant pastor" and Orchard Lake alumnus of New Britain, Connecticut. He was followed by an honor roll of clergy, lay professionals, and fraternal leaders who had received an immigrant Polish heritage and nurtured an ethnic Polish-American identity.

Above: General Tadeusz Bór-Komorowksi (front center), commander-in-chief of Polish Underground Forces during World War II, visiting the refugee "Boys from Poland" studying at St. Mary's Preparatory in 1945. The rector, Rt. Rev. Edward Szumal, stands to the general's right. *Below:* The combined forces of the Orchestra, Schola Cantorum, College Choir, and High School Glee Club under Rev. Henry Waraksa's direction in 1944.

This and opposite page: Images and descriptions of College and Seminary life in the 1950s (from the College Catalog for 1959-1960).

Prayer is the essence and mainstay of the Seminarian's life. At Orchard Lake a rosary at Our Lady's Grotto is an all-important facet of spiritual growth.

Hours of concentrated study equip the Seminarian with the knowledge which must be his as a Priest.

Devotion to Mary as promoted by the Sodality is but one of the many spiritual, cultural, and intellectual activities afforded the Seminarian at Orchard Lake.

Recreation is a never to be neglected part of a Seminarian's day mid the ample time and facilities provided at Saint Mary's.

Most Rev. John F. Dearden, Archbishop of Detroit, presents the Fidelitas Medal to Sister Mary Alexander, Mother General of the Felician Sisters, as Rt. Rev. Msgr. Wallace Filipowicz (rector from 1956 to 1967) looks on.

Above: His Eminence Karol Cardinal Wojtyła being welcomed to the campus in 1969 with a torchlight reception. Below: Rev. Walter Ziemba (rector from 1967 to 1977) speaking at the Catholic University of Lublin at its fiftieth anniversary celebration in 1968.

Opposite page: Cardinal Wojtyła and others leaving the Shrine Chapel during the conference of 1976.

Above: Pope John Paul II and Rev. Stanley Milewski (chancellor since 1977) at the Vatican in 1978. Right: Cardinal Wojtyła and his barber, Gene Seets, in 1976.

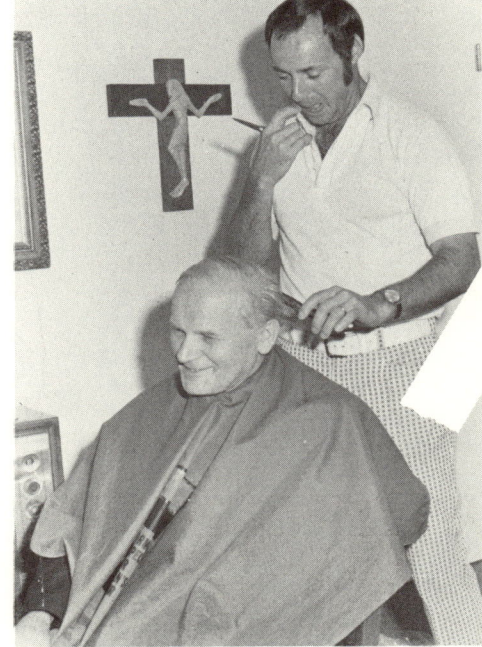

This and opposite page: Images of campus life in the late 1970s and 1980s.

Aeriel view of the campus in the 1970s.

V. *Unity Without Uniformity, 1965-1985*

THE Orchard Lake Schools were founded in a young, industrializing society to serve working class immigrants by preparing some of their sons for the priesthood and providing others with basic high school education. They succeeded in making the transition to a mature, industrial society by adapting to and even anticipating the ethnic era in the Polish-American community. The Polish-Americanization of the three schools during the first half of the twentieth century witnessed the development of a college program (which even in its heyday as a college seminary retained an identity as a college), a curriculum which incorporated the fundamentals of American education as well as the English language, a strong alumni constituency oriented to the professional and business worlds as well as to pastoral care in working class suburbs, and an elaborate mission to America through heightened self-awareness as Polish-American Catholics.

The community which created and supported the schools survived into a third, fourth, and sometimes even fifth generation by the 1980s. It was much changed by then, however; and the traditional, populous, institutionally strong neighborhoods had become relatively a smaller part of Polish America. Detroit Polonia, for example, the one with which Orchard Lake interacted most, underwent rapid change. By the end of the 1970s, many of the neighborhoods of the immigrant generation were virtually unrecognizable as Polish. They were occupied by newcomers, mainly Blacks from the rural South as well as new immigrants like Arabs, Albanians, and Yugoslavs.

The mayoralty of the Polish American Roman Gribbs in 1967-71 was both a political coming of age and a last hurrah for Polish Detroit. Especially after the riots of 1968, the speed of social change accelerated. During the seventies Detroit became a largely Black city governed by a Black political organization and ringed by expanding white suburbs. Some areas of intermediate Polish settlement, such as Hamtramck, survived as families passed their homes from one generation to another. Even they found their traditional economic base transformed between 1975 and 1985, as old auto works—like Dodge Main—were vacated or leveled and sometimes replaced by more efficient plants. Meanwhile, the more subtly ethnic suburbs expanded west and northeast while the worker suburbs of the 1950s, Warren and Sterling Heights for example, became home increasingly to the middle aged and the retired.

As third and fourth generations came to predominate among American Poles, a rapid jump in their educational level suggested a striking movement into the business-professional classes. Aside from the small but significant number of recent arrivals, younger Polish Americans (now really Americans of Polish heritage) had grown up with the ethnic memory of Poland as a backward, agricultural nation of peasants. The product of immigrants trying to explain their immigration and of an absence of contact with the old country since 1939, that image of Poland caught up with assimilated American Poles in a repression of their past and a dreary stereotyping of them by other Americans. The reopening of Poland to ordinary cultural contacts in the 1970s did much to change that view among Polish Americans although it usually confirmed in their minds the wisdom of their parents' decision to emigrate. Major events in world history—the election of a Polish pope, Nobel prizes for Czesław Miłosz and Lech Wałęsa, and the movement for peaceful social change in Poland through Solidarity—rectified the old stereotype or made it irrelevant. The emigration of Polish professionals, artists, and intellectuals to America in the aftermath of Solidarity was a further reminder of how far Poles as well as Polish Americans had assimilated to the post-industrial world of the 1980s.

If younger Polish American Catholics were better off, better educated, and more self-assured by 1980, they were also more likely than their parents to question the authority of their Church. The Second Vatican Council had indeed, in Pope John XXIII's metaphor, opened the windows of the Church to the modern age. Many found the view unsettling. American Catholics at first thought the Council would have little impact upon their daily lives. The revamping of the liturgy and the use of vernacular languages like Polish (introduced promptly in Detroit's Polish parishes) appeared to be mere cosmetic changes.

More important, the legitimacy of informed individual conscience, underscored by the Council, eventually seemed in conflict with the teaching authority of the Church. Theological exploration of time-honored beliefs and practices was encouraged. Embodied in the basic Council documents was a concept of the Church as the People of God that gave greater significance to the laity, promoted collegiality among bishops, and moderated the power of the hierarchy. Clearly, traditional Catholic teachings and the authority of the church hierarchy were not meant to be undermined, but reconciling the claims of conscience and magisterium engaged the attention of Catholics as it had not for centuries. Still, two decades after the close of the Council it was problematic whether the interior personal renewal, which would make the new views workable, had taken place among the mass of Catholics.

Open discussion of the meaning for Orchard Lake of the new demography and of Catholic renewal was initiated in 1965 by a proposal to admit college students who had no intention of pursuing a priestly vocation. A formal break with the policy of over twenty years was rejected twice; but soon after the appointment of Father Ziemba as Rector-President, he and the new Dean of the College, Father Leonard Chrobot, initiated the process which led to the admission of non-divinity students in the fall of 1969. One year later, the first women, part-time commuters majoring in theology and Polish, were admitted to college classes; and three years after that college women were resident on campus.

The debate about the admission of non-divinity students was probably moot by the time it began. Even in the era of the divinity school in 1958-1968, only 42% of the College's graduates went into the priesthood while 58% chose other occupations and careers. The decision to admit lay students still presumed that priestly formation would dominate in the College program, albeit in a new way. The Vatican Council and the new Program for Priestly Formation of the National Conference of Catholic Bishops opened the way to freer admissions and curriculum policies. Undergraduate preparation for priesthood did not now necessarily focus on a philosophy major. It emphasized instead the formation of the "liberally educated person, committed to Christ and to the service of his neighbor."

The Seminary followed a parallel course. The introduction of a program for the permanent diaconate under the leadership of the Dean, Father Anthony Kośnik, expanded the mission of the Seminary beyond priestly formation. The admission of women to the graduate programs in theology and religious education in the 1970s underscored the change. Persistent and sometimes critical softness in enrollment because of a decline in priestly vocations and the assimilation of the ethnic Polish community argued steadily for a broader student base. Gradually the College evolved a curriculum in which priestly formation was not dominant. By 1976, the number of students oriented to lay vocations outnumbered those in priestly formation; and in 1983, the students in the Priestly Formation Program were moved, at least provisionally, from the dormitory of the new College to residence in the Seminary building.

The growing number of commuter and non-traditional

students further changed the character of the College population. By 1985, they were a majority if one simply counted heads, though still less than half the full-time and full-time equivalent student totals. In any case, most students, resident or not, lived within a few hours driving distance of the campus. Over a span of fifteen years, a male, white, residential, Polish American, Roman Catholic College Seminary drawing students from throughout the Middle West and Northeast transformed itself into a lay college where women, non-whites, and foreign-born approached national norms. Only the core of full-time students remained heavily Catholic and significantly (though still a minority) Polish in heritage.

The Preparatory, the last bastion of male, residential life, also drew more heavily on non-Poles from nearby suburbs. The closed campus of old was modified to permit commuting home on most weekends, however; and the admission of day students in 1985, the first since the early days in Detroit, raised the possibility of further change. The Seminary, by way of its graduate programs, resembled and probably anticipated the College in the sex, age, and ethnic composition of its students. Paradoxically, in the 1980s, it also offered the lone, powerful exception on campus to the rule of Americanizing and commuterizing student bodies. The inability of seminaries in Poland to take all qualified priesthood candidates and the continuing need for Polish-speaking priests in America encouraged SS. Cyril and Methodius to accept mature Polish seminarians to complete their theology, learn English, and find places in American dioceses. The proportion of native Poles increased well beyond what it had been in the heyday of the "Polish" Seminary, but the greater sensitivity of American bishops to Polish affairs and the needs of ethnic communities argued strongly for their admission.

Altered student bodies required expanded or revised curricula and services. The College at first built upon membership in the Detroit Consortium of Catholic Colleges and the elaboration of majors in traditional areas, (Polish, Theology, Communication Arts, Philosophy) which required minimal investment in new staff and facilities. The Religious Education major in 1976 followed that pattern. Accreditation by the North Central States Association, a process begun in 1968 and achieved in 1976, and the shift in the student body about the same time laid the groundwork for further change. In the late 1970s and early 1980s, majors were added in Science (Biology, Chemistry, and Radiologic Technology), Business Administration, Social Science, Human Services, Computer Science, and Psychology. General education requirements were modified somewhat to accommodate the demands of career oriented majors.

College administrative services grew concurrently. The first full-time Admissions Director was appointed in 1970. A Financial Aid Office became important when the College was certified as a non-divinity school and became eligible for greater federal student aid. Though the position had various names, the equivalent of a Dean of Women was needed in the now co-educational environment. A full-time Academic Dean was appointed in 1979 to supervise instruction. The Seminary-College Registrar was separated from the Office of the Procurator-Treasurer in 1981 and converted into a full-time position two years later. Offices for Career Planning and non-traditional students in 1982-1983 fleshed out a conventional college administrative structure.

The Seminary followed a parallel path through the post-conciliar era. As vocations to the priesthood and from the Polish American community declined almost without interruption, the Seminary responded within the framework of experimentation encouraged by Vatican II. Outreach, lay ministry, and graduate programs made it a pioneer in religious education. The Center for Pastoral Studies, founded in 1968, formulated an ambitious plan for continuing education. Within a year it had launched one of the first full-time programs for the permanent diaconate in the United States. Success encouraged imitation on a part-time basis in diocesan seminaries; and the full-time programs were phased out eventually. The impulse to prepare laity, including women, for ministry took other new forms. A Master's in Theology, offered jointly with the University of Detroit in

1970, and a Master of Divinity degree in 1974, served the needs of lay students as well as the continuing education of clergy. The Master of Divinity was also a terminal degree for students moving through the Seminary toward ordination. A Master's program in Religious Education in 1977 trained teachers in a field being rapidly transformed by the decline in teaching congregations of sisters and of the full-service Catholic school system. A certificate program in pastoral ministry further extended the most venerable academic tradition of the Theologate. At their peak, the programs of the new Seminary enrolled more than one hundred. "Journeying in Ministry," a theology summer session, began in 1979 to accommodate the needs of all varieties of students in a new time frame.

Even as the Seminary reminded itself in the early 1980s of its primary mission—the formation of priests—and embarked upon a Polish American Vocation Awareness Program and a formal recruitment program, even then the programmatic innovations of the sixties and seventies remained attractively in place. The return to "basics" in the 1980s was formally apparent in the appointment of directors of spiritual formation and admissions, and in a surge of applications from Polish-born and Polish-trained seminarians who wished to complete their formation at Orchard Lake. The trend, at least for the moment, raised the possibility of a "Polish" seminary that even Father Dąbrowski had not contemplated.

The Polish American Liturgical Center, founded in 1971, energetically and with great success also adapted and expanded upon the traditional pastoral mission in Polish of the Seminary. The missalette *Pan z wami,* its major publication, reached a circulation of 60,000 in 1985 by offering the Catholic liturgy in Polish to parishes and individual subscribers in more than 16 countries. *Słowo i Liturgia,* its other publication with a circulation of 300, assisted priests in the preparation of Polish-language homilies. The outlines of the neo-Polish seminary that emerged by the mid-1980s were confirmed in the perceptions of bishops of dioceses that had received large numbers of graduates from Orchard Lake. SS.

Cyril and Methodius, they believed, had a solid record of achievement during the immigrant and ethnic eras; the need for Polish-speaking priests had appeared to decline from the 1950s to the 1970s; but the special pastoral needs of old Polish Americans as well as recent immigrants was still significant; and the power of ethnic parishes to act as cohesive social forces, regardless of the number of Polish speakers, merited the formation of priests sensitive to Polish and Polish American sensibilities.

The High School at Orchard Lake underwent no major curricular change in this period—it was bound by the expectations of colleges and by state standards—though greater variety was introduced into its offerings, particularly as it prepared for the admission in 1985 of non-resident students. The faculty and administration of the High School were deeply affected, however, by the drive to improve credentials and by the challenge to authoritarianism throughout Catholic education during the 1960s and 1970s. In order to retain its license as a boarding school in 1960, the High School arranged to have its teachers formally certified at the secondary level.

More significant, since it affected instructional budgeting and a time-honored personnel policy, was the challenge to the practice of using the same faculty in each school. As the College prepared for accreditation in the late 1960s, it was clear that the North Central Association expected the College faculty to be divorced from the High School, whatever the increased cost and loss of good teachers in the High School might be. The prospect of accreditation also encouraged the establishment of the principle of teaching within one's area of expertise, normal work loads, and widely accepted policies on rank and status embodied in the first College Faculty Handbook. Both the College and Seminary sought to increase the number of faculty with terminal degrees in the disciplines they taught; and a significant number of women, many of them religious, joined the staffs and faculties of the three schools for the first time in the 1970s. In a parallel administrative development, the Business

Office also modernized its bookkeeping and handling of accounts during the 1960s.

Inevitably, changing student bodies, curricula, and faculties were reflected in the physical plant. In 1971, the High School occupied a new residence hall where it also established its own library. College women, initially housed in a small frame house at the edge of campus, replaced the prepsters in the Barracks as their number unexpectedly grew in 1973. They shared the Barracks with the now more diverse resident faculty while other portions of the building were converted to faculty offices and laboratories.

All that paled, however, beside the "reorientation of faculty and personnel thinking" that one report predicted would be more important than adjusting to administrative or physical changes. Nowhere was the required reorientation more evident than in the area of discipline, now subsumed under the term "student life." Orchard Lake had long been a way of life, a process of formation, in which academic achievement was only one part, and not always the most important part at that. The social and personal code that governed had never been monolithic in practice, but it had been widely accepted as the public standard. The old regulations gave way in 1965-1967 in the College Seminary to new ways and a new spirit which only a much later generation of students found modest. Radios were permitted in dormitory rooms, and private cars were allowed on campus, two signs of a recreational style and physical mobility to come.

Predictably, the admission of lay college students was associated with more visible changes in life style—the elimination of curfews, permissions to leave campus, compulsory attendance at campus functions (especially liturgies), and prohibitions against alcohol at student social functions. Experiments with student government, parietal hours, and new forms of social interaction marked the late 1970s. As clear a sign of change as any, varsity college basketball was reintroduced in 1974 with a limited schedule. Players were primarily St. Mary's students with an avocation. After 1978, the college inaugurated a more ambitious program to recruit players who would also attend St. Mary's, hired a stronger coaching staff, adopted a more competitive schedule, and joined several small college conferences and athletic associations. The hope was that achievement in the sport would modify the College's image as a divinity school and in so doing attract and retain students.

The Seminary was affected to some degree by the trend toward traditional college student life, but the maturity and career goals of seminarians rendered much of it irrelevant. The High School lagged behind in the reformation of authoritarian discipline, probably because of the youth of its students; but it too finally adopted a constructive approach based as much on persuasion, counseling, and the influence of peers as on supervision and regulations. The end of obligatory attendance at daily mass and permission to commute home most weekends were only the most visible signs of a new order and the changed expectations of parents in the 1980s.

The social and academic reorientation of the Orchard Lake Schools in the 1970s coincided with administrative reorganization somewhat like that between 1927 and 1942. Its purposes were to give more autonomy to each school, professionalize administration, improve the oversight capability of regents and trustees, and expand the financial base of the institution. The formal decision to seek accreditation for St. Mary's College in 1968 focused everyone's attention on those goals. As a first step, in 1971, the Board of Trustees replaced itself and the old Corporation with a Board of Regents. Ex-officio membership in the new Board was largely the same as in the old: the Catholic Archbishop of Detroit, major administrators, alumni, and Polonia leaders. Otherwise, the Board was open to "any person of proven good will and dedication" to its purposes. Separate boards of control were drawn from the Regents for each of the Schools: a Board of Directors for the Preparatory, a Board of Trustees for the College, and a Board of Consultants chaired by the Archbishop of Detroit for the Seminary.

The resignation of Rev. Walter Ziemba as Rector-President-Superintendent in June 1977 set the stage for the logical next step. Rev. Stanley Milewski succeeded him in the new post of Chancellor of the Orchard Lake Schools and Centers; a separate Rector was appointed for the Seminary; a President for the College; and a Superintendent-Principal for the Preparatory. Operations were coordinated by the Chancellor through an Executive Council composed of him, the Vice-Chancellor, and the three heads of Schools. The Chancellor participated in the deliberations of the sub-boards, supervised the Centers, and directed two combined operations: current accounts and plant through a Procurator-Treasurer (the Comptroller from 1983), and a cluster of development and fund-raising offices. Finally, the education of the Regents to their oversight function, much talked about in the 1970s, but frustrated by use of the position too often as an honorific award, was implemented in 1983, when their number, which had risen to an unwieldy 120, was reduced to 30. The boards of control in each school were reduced proportionately, and provision was made for the membership of non-Regents.

Each of the new boards and the Finance Committee of the streamlined Regents began to ask searching questions about Orchard Lake's finances. The 1970s had been no less harsh to the economy of Orchard Lake than they were to that of other schools. The opening of the Fieldhouse in 1973 unintentionally marked the end of a building era. Then, high inflation rates forced operating costs to increase more rapidly than income. A 15.5% increase in costs during 1971-1974, difficult enough to sustain, was followed by a 27% increase in 1972-1975. The Schools responded to the challenge. They had long depended almost entirely on gifts to finance themselves, and they continued to do astonishingly well at that. The established support groups—Alumni, Ladies Auxiliary, Friends, Moms and Dads—held their own and then some in the 1970s. Founder's Day, which tapped outside sources of support, reached a peak in 1979 and leveled off in the early 1980s. The Ladies' Auxiliary inaugurated its own Dinner-Party in 1970, a smaller version of the Founder's Day stag event. During the seventies, Fathers Ziemba and Milewski implemented two imaginative ideas for reaching large donors: the "Ambassadors" in 1974 to build the permanent endowment, and the Chancellor's Senate in 1978-1979 to help cover operating expenses. Raffles, lotteries, bingo, and games of chance also played a large part in all fund raisers, notably Founder's Day, and in the expansion of smaller new events such as the Moms and Dads' Christmas Fair in November and the Polish Country Fair in May.

On several occasions the Schools had experimented with public relations or advertising agencies, notably in expanding the Friends campaign in the 1950s and in promoting "Project: Pole" in 1971. In 1978, they established a continuing relationship with the first of several financial development firms in suburban Detroit. A professionally mounted, twenty-seven million dollar capital fund drive, timed to coincide with the Centennial in 1985, grew out of those experiences. Meanwhile, the Schools shored up the more conventional base of their operating budgets. Active recruitment of students outside the old alumni network took on new significance. Tuition and fees were made to bear a larger portion of costs without, it was hoped, sacrificing the historic commitment to less well-off students. The ability of the College to receive gifts, which were tax-deductible under Michigan law, facilitated fund raising. Federal work study moneys also became available to the College in 1972, as well as all other kinds of public grants and guaranteed student loans in 1975 when the College was certified as primarily a non-divinity school.

The challenge of post-industrial society to an institution rooted in old world America prompted Orchard Lake to search the depths of its collective soul. Had the success of three-quarters of a century made the schools unable to succeed in a world which was less Polish and less Catholic in traditional terms? The fatalism so characteristic of traditional Polish Catholic thinking did not prevail, however; instead the Orchard Lake leadership chose to reintegrate the Schools with the world of the late twentieth century.

Polishness at Orchard Lake was again the most sensitive barometer of change. Polish continued to be spoken by a large number of priest faculty and administrators. Indeed it may have grown stronger as the number of native Poles increased in the middle 1980s in both the faculty and the student body of the Seminary and in the staff of the plant and maintenance department. The transmission of the language to another generation of Americans was another question. It was by no means an impossible task as the success of some students with no Polish background indicated. After years of desultory debate about "the negative attitude towards Polish," the plain truth that Polish was a foreign language for nearly all students was accepted frankly as the basis of instruction. What were perceived as "legalistic" teaching styles and "archaic methods which alienate our youth" were swept aside between 1965 and 1970. Trained language instructors were hired in the College and Preparatory; a language laboratory was installed; curricular materials were developed in cooperation with specialists at Ann Arbor and eventually at Orchard Lake itself; and students were encouraged to enter summer language and cultural programs in Poland. Above all, the reformed program sought to motivate students with a brighter and more youthful image of Polish culture. As late as 1985, it was still possible to take eleven consecutive years of instruction in Polish from the Preparatory where it was required for two years through the Theologate where it was required of all men preparing for service in Polish American parishes.

Orchard Lake's external "Polish" task was "to become the intellectual, spiritual and cultural center of the American Polonia," the place where American Polonia did its thinking. The Center for Polish Studies and Culture was founded in 1968 as the centerpiece of that effort in education broadly conceived. Over the next fifteen years Orchard Lake created an array of programs oriented to off-campus Polish audiences—a Polish Day on the first Sunday of each month, an artist-in-residence and a significant gallery of Polish art, a weekly Polish radio mass, an accessible and catalogued library collection of some 8,000 Polish books, a professionally managed Archives of Polonia and Orchard Lake materials, reference publications on Polish Studies and

Polish American life, subsidies to students engaged in Polish Studies, the Pope John Paul II Center for collecting printed material and memorabilia on the Polish pope, the Polish American Sports Hall of Fame, a popular diorama of Polish history and culture, and a concert series, not to mention films and lectures as the occasion arose. The first Polish American Heritage Workshop in the summer of 1976 focused attention on the American consequences of Polishness.

Orchard Lake's role as a Polonian spiritual center was evident in the emerging dialogue between the Polish and American churches. Meetings between the Polish and Polish American bishops at the Second Vatican Council, the commemoration of Poland's millenium on both sides of the Atlantic, and numerous individual contacts culminating in the visits of His Eminence Karol Cardinal Wojtyła in 1969 and 1976, finally ended the post-war separation of the Polish Church and its ethnic American offspring. The visit of eighteen Polish bishops and Cardinal Wojtyła in August, 1976, formalized Orchard Lake's role as a gateway for Poles into America. By the conclusion of their symposium Polish and Polish American church leaders arrived at a consensus regarding the Polish pastorate in the United States. The new immigrants required a new approach, probably the ministry of native speakers of Polish who were comfortable with contemporary Polish life, if they were to be served by the American Church.

Beyond the relatively small number of recent immigrants, a Polish pastorate was needed, according to Cardinal Wojtyła, "since it is well known that one does not merely belong to a nation on the basis of the spoken language. Possibly the most important element is national identity, since the feeling of cultural belonging is much more profound than a familiarity with the language. We can be easily convinced of this by our meetings with representatives of the second or third generation who speak Polish poorly or not at all, yet in whom it is still easy to trace the cultural heritage of Poland."[1] In order to deal with the multi-cultural Polonia the assembly of priests and bishops agreed on varieties of exchange between the United States and Poland ranging from information and personal contacts to students at seminaries.

The visit of the Polish bishops illustrated the third function of Orchard Lake's Polishness, bridging the cultural divide between Old World and assimilated Americans. Orchard Lake would, in Father Ziemba's words, put Americans in personal contact "with the values we represent as Americans of Polish background." In this updating of the Polish American Catholic mission, Orchard Lake renders "service to all Americans but particularly the Poles and Americans of Polish background as they search for a new way to find what it means to be an American."[2] One of those new ways of being American was summarized by Father Chrobot, possibly the chief popularizer of the new ethnicity among Polish Americans: "Orchard Lake upholds the goal of true unity without absolute uniformity, demanding the right to individual differences in a culturally pluralistic society."[3]

Briefly in the late 1960s, it seemed as though the mountain had come to Mohammed. Orchard Lake was a significant participant in the Black-Polish Conference which tried to heal communal relations in the aftermath of the great Detroit riot of 1968. Twice, in 1969 and 1970, the campus was the site of Conferences on Cultural Pluralism through which Orchard Lake's traditional social philosophy and curricular plans in Polish won wide attention. A decade later it was the founding locale of the National Polish American-Jewish American Task Force, a contemporary reminder of one of Europe's oldest cross-cultural relationships.

Orchard Lake's most public effort "to protect the true image of the Pole and Polish-American" and implicitly to offer a model for the new ethnicity occurred in 1970-1971. It was born of discontent with the uncoordinated character and limited reach of traditional Polish American public relations. Buoyed by the support of Leo Stein, the Schools took ads in *Life* and *Newsweek* in June, 1970. Then, with the aid of Philadelphia businessman Edward Piszek, they participated in a media blitz, "Project: POLE," in the fall of 1971. Books, posters, and other publications were designed to present a variety of mass audiences with the Polish and Polish American story. Inserts were placed in major American as well as ethnic Polish newspapers. Press interviews, an appearance by Father Ziemba and Mr. Piszek on national television, a visit to Senator Edmund Muskie (at the moment a leading contender for a Presidential nomination) were contrived to create an event whose message was that Polish Americans were no longer immigrants or inhabitants of an ethnic ghetto but had begun in great number to join the mainstream of American life.

Cardinal Wojtyła's thoughtful response to what he heard about Polonia during his visit of 1976 continued the long dialogue between the Polish past and the Polish American present at Orchard Lake. Like many before him, he had an apocalyptic vision of western civilization in which Poland played a special part:

> We are now facing the final confrontation between the Church and the anti-Church, of the Gospel versus the anti-Gospel. . . . We all realize it is not an easy matter, and a great deal of it depends upon the outcome on the Vistula. I think that Polonia is perhaps the most aware of it, and it seems to me that other layers of American society are less enlightened in this respect and simply eliminate this problem from their sphere of interests. Polonia, which shares Poland's sentiments, feels the significance of the confrontation going on at the banks of the Vistula. It is a trial of not only our nation and Church, but in a sense a test of two thousand years culture and Christian civilization with all its consequences for human dignity, individual rights, human rights, and the rights of nations. As the number of people who understand the importance of this confrontation increase in Poland and America, we can look with greater trust towards the outcome of this confrontation. The Church has gone through many trials, as has the Polish nation, and has emerged victorious even though at a cost of great sacrifice.[4]

The trials of the Polish nation and Church, the Cardinal from Kraków believed, were major factors in depriving the immigrant of support in establishing himself more solidly in the new society. Unlike many American leaders of the new ethnicity, Wojtyła refused to shift major responsibility for the slow social progress of Polish immigrants to more Americanized ethnic groups. Poles had to accept their own history, including, in the case of Polonia, some of the blame for the loss of the mother tongue. That history may account for their assimilation: "Polonia is a community which lives, survives and acts under American conditions and within the confines of American society." Nevertheless, the Cardinal acknowledged a profound moral loss within the framework of his personalist philosophy: "This process of external assimilation which Polonia underwent, is in a sense morally negative since it may signify the negation of oneself which man should not allow to happen . . . Were I to compare it [the search for identity] to the sphere of spiritual guidance, it would have to be a very personal guidance since it is a question of awakening one's awareness and conscience and bringing to life one's personal responsibility." Finally, he refused to engage in hand-wringing about the past: "we should not stop at considering simply how much we have acquired, but rather how much we have achieved in view of the underprivileged state in which Polonia originally found itself."[5] The passage of time would bring what the burden of Polish history had made difficult to achieve at first.

The Orchard Lake Schools had been both consequence and cause of the history that Cardinal Wojtyła invoked to help his audience to meet the present and prepare for the future. As the Schools approached their second century, they had educated upwards of 15,000 students and 2,300 priests who had transformed the communities that had generated and sustained the Schools. Centenaries are, after all, arbitrary units of time imposed by the human compulsion to order our memories. History has its own rhythms. The Polish Seminary and the allied Schools at Orchard Lake have measured their time in response to the development of immigrant Poles and their children, first as they carved out a place for themselves in America, then as they defined themselves as Catholic Polish Americans. Many of the issues they confronted and much of the vocabulary they used in 1985 might still sound familiar to Father Dąbrowski were he to appear at the Lake in 1985. The size, complexity, and novelties of the Schools, not to mention of America, in the 1980s would both surprise and please him. Their challenge would stimulate him. The continuing emphasis on values-oriented education, on formation really, and the sense that the Schools represent something distinctively larger than themselves would comfort the Founder. Moored in the belief that "Intelligence only can make men free," Father Dąbrowski and his spiritual heirs would confront their tradition and their future. Like Cardinal Wojtyła in 1976, they might cite Stanisław Wyspiański who said that "Poles could have more if they would only will to want it." "Maybe," they would add as the then future pope did, "we have changed enough so that Poles will want more; if only they want more, they will be able to have more."[6]

Bibliographical Note

As the perspicacious reader familiar with the Orchard Lake Schools will immediately realize, this history rests upon secondary, printed works generated by the Schools themselves for the bulk of its factual content. Three of these works were occasioned by previous anniversaries. Two were prepared by a long-time member of the faculty, Andrew Piwowarski: *Historya Seminaryum Polskiego w Detroit i Orchard Lake, Mich. z Okazyi 25-letniego Jubileuszu. 1910* (Detroit?, 1910?); and *Almanach Jubileuszowy Seminarjum Polskiego Kolegjum Św. Marji i Szkoły Wyższej w Orchard Lake, Michigan* (Detroit, 1935). The third was edited by Leonard F. Chrobot, then a student, under the general direction of Rev. Walter Ziemba as part of the diamond jubilee yearbook. It was reprinted separately as: *Seventy-Five Years of the Orchard Lake Seminary* (Orchard Lake, 1960).

The major critical history of Seminary, which takes the story through 1903, is Joseph Swastek's "The Formative Years of the Polish Seminary in the United States," in *Sacrum Poloniae Millenium,* 6 (Rome, 1959), 39-149, reprinted by the Center for Polish Studies and Culture of the Orchard Lake Schools in 1985. It contains an extensive bibliography. For the period since 1903, I was able to consult the major publications of the Seminary and the Schools— *Niedziela, Sodalis, Alumnus, Lake Oracle, Good News,* catalogs since 1920, and yearbooks from 1928 to 1977. The minutes of faculty and administrative meetings are available from the 1940s. Still, they are only a fraction of what is available in the Orchard Lake Archives and in various offices on campus.

The recollections of persons associated with the Schools are acknowledged in the preface. They provided additional material and, more important, suggested perspectives on the past and significance in the facts. I also relied heavily on Norman Davies' *God's Playground* (2 vols.; New York; Columbia University Press, 1982) for an overview of Polish history. The work of many American scholars, mostly of Polish descent, who have succeeded in recovering a large part of the Polish American past since the 1960s, also provided indispensable background and insights. It was possible to mention only a few of them in chapter notes that serve mainly to identify the sources of quotations.

CHAPTER NOTES

CHAPTER I

1. The meaning of "Polonia," the Latin term for Poland, is ambiguous. Assimilated to the Polish language, it came in the twentieth century to refer increasingly to any organized, consciously Polish community living outside European Poland. It is possible, therefore, to speak of Chicago Polonia, American Polonia, or World Polonia. As immigrant or ethnic communities dispersed and lost their coherence with the passage of time, "Polonia" has frequently been used to describe all those of Polish heritage, occasionally including persons who are no longer conscious of their Polish descent.

2. Stanislaus A. Blejwas, "The Origins and Practice of 'Organic Work' in Poland," *The Polish Review,* 15:4 (1970), 23.

CHAPTER II

1. Joseph V. Swastek, "The Formative Years of the Polish Seminary in the United States," in *Sacrum Poloniae Millenium,* 6 (Rome, 1959), 98.

2. Joseph J. Parot, *Polish Catholics in Chicago, 1850-1920* (DeKalb, Ill., 1981), pp. 20-21.

3. Sr. Mary Janice Ziółkowski, CSSF, *The Felician Sisters of Livonia, Michigan* (Detroit, 1984), p. 51.

4. Swastek, "The Formative Years," p. 52.

5. Swastek, "The Formative Years," p. 54.

6. Thaddeus C. Radzialowski, "Reflections on the History

of the Felicians in America," *Polish American Studies,* 32:1 (1975), 24 note.
  7. Radzialowski, p. 23.
  8. Joseph V. Swastek, "Drugi List Publiczny Ks. Dąbrowskiego w Sprawie Założenia Seminarium" ["Father Dąbrowski's Second Public Letter on the Occasion of the Founding of the Seminary"], *Sodalis,* 40:4 (1959), 99. The author is indebted to Mr. Robert Geryk for the translation.
  9. Swastek, "Drugi List," p. 100.
  10. Aleksander Syski, *Ks. Józef Dąbrowski* (Orchard Lake, 1942), p. 136.
  11. Swastek, "The Formative Years," p. 60.
  12. Swastek, "The Formative Years," p. 62.
  13. *Detroit Free Press,* July 23, 1885.
  14. Swastek, "The Formative Years," p. 115.
  15. *Detroit Free Press,* July 23, 1885.
  16. Joseph V. Swastek, "Początki Seminarium Polskiego w Świetle Publicznych Listów Księdza Dąbrowskiego" ["The Beginnings of the Polish Seminary in the Public Letters of Father Dąbrowski"], *Sodalis,* 40:3 (1959), 89.
  17. Swastek, "The Formative Years," p. 126.
  18. Swastek, "The Formative Years," p. 127.
  19. Swastek, "The Formative years," p. 111.
  20. *Detroit News,* January 30, 1903.
  21. Swastek, "The Formative Years," p. 114.
  22. Swastek, "The Formative Years," p. 100.
  23. Swastek, "The Formative Years," p. 92.

CHAPTER III

  1. C.H. Oldfather and Alphonse M. Schwitalla, "Report of the Board of Review of Commission on Institutions of Higher Education, North Central Association of Colleges and Secondary Schools" (1941), p. 11. Copy in St. Mary's College, Accreditation File.
  2. Oldfather and Schwitalla, p.3.
  3. Joseph A. Gierut to Daniel M. O'Connell, October 21, 1937, in St. Mary's College, Accreditation File.
  4. *The Eagle* (1959), p. 169.
  5. Andrew Piwowarski, *Almanach Jubileuszowy Seminarjum Polskiego Kolegjum Św. Marji i Szkoły Wyższej w Orchard Lake, Michigan [Jubilee Almanac of the Polish Seminary, St.*

Mary's College and High School in Orchard Lake, Michigan] (Detroit, 1935), p. 213. (Trans: Hej comrades, hej alumni from the Polish Seminary/Let us all be proud that we are the descendants of Lech.)

6. Leonard F. Chrobot, ed., *Seventy-Five Years of the Orchard Lake Seminary* (Orchard Lake, 1960), pp. 86, 87.

7. Oldfather and Schwitalla, p. 3.

CHAPTER IV

1. Stanislaus Blejwas, "Old and New Polonias: Tensions within an Ethnic Community," *Polish American Studies*, 38:2 (1981), 57.

2. Valerius Jasiński, "A Polish Seminary in Contemporary America," *The Homiletic and Pastoral Review*, 41 (October, 1940), 27-28.

3. *The Eagle* (1946), unpaged.

4. Jasiński, p. 28.

5. Jasiński, p. 28.

6. Joseph V. Swastek, "What Is a Polish American?" *Polish American Studies*, 1 (1944), 38.

7. Swastek, "What Is a Polish American?" p. 40.

8. Swastek, "What Is a Polish American?" p. 40.

9. Jasiński, pp. 30, 33.

10. Oldfather and Schwitalla, p. 28.

11. Jasiński, pp. 31-32.

12. Jasiński, p. 32.

13. Chrobot, pp. 53, 54.

14. Chrobot, p. 54.

CHAPTER V

1. *Kosciuszko Foundation Newsletter*, 31:2 (1976-77), 11.

2. Walter J. Ziemba, " 'Project: POLE': Its Significance," Typescript in author's possession of paper read at Annual Convention of the American Council of Polish Cultural Clubs, June 15, 1972, p. 2.

3. St. Mary's College, *A Report of the College's Self-Study Submitted to the North Central Association* (1976), p. 17.

4. *Kosciuszko Foundation Newsletter*, pp. 11-12.

5. *Kosciuszko Foundation Newsletter*, pp. 9-10.

6. *Kosciuszko Foundation Newsletter*, p. 12.

APPENDIX:

CHRONICLE OF IMPORTANT EVENTS IN THE HISTORIES OF AMERICA, POLAND, POLISH AMERICA, AND THE POLISH SEMINARY.

Date	POLAND	AMERICA/ UNITED STATES	POLISH AMERICA	POLISH SEMINARY/ ORCHARD LAKE SCHOOLS
966	Prince Mieszko and Polish leadership converted to Roman Catholic Christianity			
1079	Assassination of Stanislaus, Bishop of Kraków			
1226	Teutonic Knights join Poles in conquest of Prussians			
1241	First Mongol invasion			
1264	First formal protection for Jews in Poland			
1364	Foundation of University of Kraków			
1386	Personal union of Poland and Lithuania (marriage of Jadwiga and Jagiełło)			
1410	Poles defeat Teutonic Knights at Grunwald			
1492		Columbus' first voyage to America		
1493	**First Seym (Parliament) to legislate for Poland as a whole**			

1543	Publication of Copernicus' *On the Revolution of the Heavenly Bodies*	
1569	Union of Lublin joins Poland and Lithuania in a single state and establishes elective kingship	
1607	English colony at Jamestown, Virginia	
1608		First Poles at Jamestown
1612	Polish army in Moscow; apogee of Poland's international power	
1620		English colony at Plymouth, and Mayflower Compact
1628		Puritan English colony in Massachusetts
1648	Ukrainian rebellion against Polish rule	
1655	Swedish occupation of Poland and siege of Częstochowa	
1683	King John Sobieski leads defense of Vienna against Turks	

Date	POLAND	AMERICA/ UNITED STATES	POLISH AMERICA	POLISH SEMINARY/ ORCHARD LAKE SCHOOLS
1689		Opening of first Anglo-French colonial war (to 1697)		
1763		English assume control of Canada and all of eastern North America from France		
1772	First partition of Poland by Prussia, Russia, and Austria			
1775		Opening of Revolutionary War (to 1783)		
1776		Declaration of Independence	Thaddeus Kościuszko arrives to participate in American Revolutionary army	
1779			Death of Casimir Pulaski at Savannah	
1787		Constitutional Convention		
1791	"Third of May" Constitution; efforts to renew Polish nation			
1794	Insurrection and war with Russia led by Kościuszko			
1795	Third partition and disappearance of Polish state			

1797			Kościuszko in U.S. (to 1798)
1812	War with England (to 1815)		
1815	Congress of Vienna establishes division of Poland through 1918		
1823	Beginning of end of serfdom in Prussian Poland (completed in 1850s)	Monroe Doctrine	
1830	Major insurrection in Russian Poland (suppressed in 1831)		
1834			First significant group of refugees from insurrection of 1830-31 arrive in New York
1842			Joseph Dąbrowski born
1846	Disturbances in Austrian Poland lead to end of serfdom by 1848	War with Mexico (to 1848) and territorial expansion	
1850		Sectional crisis and compromise on expansion of slavery	
1854			Silesian Poles establish Panna Maria in Texas; Polish settlements follow in Midwest
1855	Death of Adam Mickiewicz		

Date	POLAND	AMERICA/ UNITED STATES	POLISH AMERICA	POLISH SEMINARY/ ORCHARD LAKE SCHOOLS
1861		Inauguration of Abraham Lincoln and beginning of Civil War	Poles participate on both sides in American Civil War	
1863	Major insurrection in Russian Poland through 1865; philosophy of organic work dominant for a generation afterward			
1864	End of serfdom in Russian Poland			
1865		End of Civil War and abolition of slavery		
1866			St. Stanislaus Kostka Society and Gmina Polska in Chicago —prototypes of Polish immigrant voluntary associations	
1867		Fourteenth, "Civil Rights" Amendment to Constitution		
1869			Foundation of Polish Roman Catholic Union of America in Detroit	
1873		Financial panic and economic depression (to 1877)		Fr. Dąbrowski arrives in U.S. (to Polonia, WI in 1870)

160

1874	Fr. Vincent Barzyński pastor of St. Stanislaus Kostka in Chicago (to 1897); Felician Sisters in America	
1879		Pope Leo XIII consents to establishment of Polish Seminary in America under direction of Rev. Leopold Moczygemba
1880	Foundation of Polish National Alliance	
1882		Felician Sisters establish headquarters in Detroit; Fr. Dąbrowski joins them as chaplain and assumes direction of Polish Seminary project
1884	Financial panic and economic depression (to 1885)	Bishop Caspar H. Borgess of Detroit grants permission to Fr. Dąbrowski to begin Seminary project
1885		Cornerstone laid for Polish Seminary building in Detroit
1886	Foundation of American Federation of Labor; Haymarket Riot in Chicago	

Date	POLAND	AMERICA/ UNITED STATES	POLISH AMERICA	POLISH SEMINARY/ ORCHARD LAKE SCHOOLS
1890			Austria and Russia replace Prussia as main sources of Polish immigration	
1891				*Niedziela (Sunday)* begins publication (to 1908)
1893	Rise of mass political parties (Socialists, National Democrats, Peasants)	Financial panic ushers in labor unrest economic depression (to 1897)		
1896		Election of President William McKinley inaugurates long era of Republican party rule		Founding of "Sons of Poland Society," later Polish Literary Society
1897			Fr. Anthony Kozlowski consecrated bishop of Independent Polish Catholics in Chicago; striking Polish miners massacred at Latimer, PA	
1898		Spanish-American War	Foundation of Polish Women's Alliance	
1900				Polish Literary Society publishes first student newspaper periodical

1903			Student protest; Fr. Dabrowski dies and is succeeded by Fr. Witold Buhaczkowski as Rector
1905	Socialist led uprising in Russian Poland		
1907		Fr. Francis Hodur consecrated bishop for Polish National Catholic Church	
1908		Fr. Paul Rhode consecrated first Roman Catholic bishop of Polish descent in U.S.	
1909			Fr. Buhaczkowski purchases site of Michigan Military Academy, and Polish Seminary moves to Orchard Lake
1910		Polish national congress in Washington, D.C.	
1913		Peak of Polish immigration (174,000 enter U.S.)	
1914	Beginning of World War I	Opening of Panama Canal; Ford Motor Co. introduces modern assembly line and five-dollar daily wage	War relief for Poland undertaken; Construction of Seminary Building (to 1916)

Date	POLAND	AMERICA/ UNITED STATES	POLISH AMERICA	POLISH SEMINARY/ ORCHARD LAKE SCHOOLS
1916				Fr. Buhaczkowksi resigns and Fr. Michael Grupa succeeds him as Rector in 1917
1917		U.S. enters European War against Germany (through 1918)	Recruitment for Polish Army in America	Sodality of Our Lady founded
1918	End of World War I; restoration of Polish state under Josef Pilsudski	Senate rejects U.S. participation in League of Nations; Prohibition Amendment to Constitution adopted		
1919	Treaty of Versailles establishes Polish western borders		Race riot in Chicago; tension between Poles and Jews; unsuccessful steel workers strike	Polish Students Mission Society organized; Scranton Student Club founded, followed by other area clubs
1920	Polish armies defeat Soviet Union			Publication of *Sodalis* begins (through 1981)
1922				Eucharistic League founded
1923				Alumni Association organized in modern form; "Golden Age" of college-seminary basketball (to 1925)

1924	Restrictive quota legislation limits immigration to U.S.		Construction of "Noah's Ark," classics dormitory and classroom building
1925			Kościuszko Foundation established
1926		Pilsudski's coup d'état inaugurates military rule	
1927			Reconstruction of "Barracks" and addition of two wings (to 1928)
1928			Reorganization of curriculum and administrative structure along "American" lines (to 1929)
1929	Financial panic followed by Great Depression (to 1940)		Orchard Lake faculty members aid in incorporating Orchard Lake Village
1930			St. Mary's recognized as degree granting college; Orchard Lake Schools reach peak enrollment of 540
			Phi Gamma Chi college fraternity founded; Championship high school basketball and college football teams (to 1933)

Date	POLAND	AMERICA/ UNITED STATES	POLISH AMERICA	POLISH SEMINARY/ ORCHARD LAKE SCHOOLS
1932		Election of President Franklin Roosevelt inaugurates long era of Democratic party predominance		Fr. Grupa resigns and Fr. Anthony Klowo is appointed Rector
1934			Second Congress of Poles Abroad in Warsaw	Major fund drive in Polish parishes in anticipation of golden jubilee
1935		Social Security Act		Felician Sisters at Orchard Lake
1936		C.I.O. launches drive to organize mass production industries		
1937				Msgr. Klowo dies and Fr. Ladislaus Krzyżosiak is appointed Rector
1938				Msgr. Stephen Woźnicki consecrated as first alumnus-bishop; *Eagle* yearbook begins publication (to 1977)
1939	Beginning of World War II; partition of Poland between Germany and Soviet Union		War relief for Poland undertaken	Ladies Auxiliary founded

1941	German invasion of Soviet Union; U.S. enters World War in alliance with Britain and Soviet Union against Japan and Germany; Polish-Soviet cooperation through 1943	Reincorporation of schools with ownership transferred from Archdiocese of Detroit to representative group of Polish American Catholic clergy and laity; construction of Marian Grotto; Faculty War Relief for Poland organized
1943	Great Power Conference at Teheran concedes eastern Polish territories to Soviet Union	Msgr. Krzyzosiak resigns and is succeeded as Rector by Fr. Edward Szumal
1944		Polish American Congress founded
1945	Yalta Conference concedes Poland to Soviet sphere of influence; end of World War II	
1947	Worsening relation with Soviet Union; Truman Doctrine	
1948	Marshall Plan to aid Europe; Communists (Polish United Workers Party) consolidates power and introduces Stalinist regime	Enactment of Displaced Persons Act inaugurates new large-scale Polish immigration to U.S.
1949	North Atlantic Treaty (U.S.-West European alliance)	"Boys from Poland"; origins of Friends of the Orchard Lake Schools

Date	POLAND	AMERICA/ UNITED STATES	POLISH AMERICA	POLISH SEMINARY/ ORCHARD LAKE SCHOOLS
1950		Korean War (to 1953)		
1953				Fidelitas Medal Award instituted; first annual Founder's Day fund-raising event
1954		Supreme Court outlaws racial segregation in public schools; acceleration of civil rights movement	Edmund Muskie elected governor of Maine	
1955	Warsaw Pact organized			
1956	Władysław Gomułka returns to power as party leader; moderation of Stalinist Policies			Msgr. Szumal dies and Fr. Wallace Filipowicz appointed Rector; construction of new Orchard Lake Post Office on school grounds
1957				Dedication of Alumni Memorial Library; foundation of Aquinas Academy, Conrad Club, and Skarga Society (through 1958)
1958				*Prep Laker*, High School publication, founded

1962			**Dedication of Shrine Chapel; construction of College Residence and Classroom Building**
1964			Founding of Knights of Dabrowski
1965	Major escalation of U.S. intervention in Vietnam War	Revision of immigration law allows entry by more Poles	
1966	Celebration of millenium of Poland's Christianity and nationhood; tension between church and government		Construction of new Dining Hall
1967	Major race riots in Detroit, Newark and (in 1968) Chicago		Msgr. Filipowicz dies and is succeeded by Fr. Walter Ziemba as Rector-President-Superintendant
1968	Election of President Richard M. Nixon heralds era of Republican party leadership	A. Mazewski succeeds C. Rozmarek as president of Polish American Congress	Center for Pastoral Studies and Center for Polish Studies and Culture founded, followed by Polish American Liturgical Center (1970) and Pope John Paul II Center (1978)
1969			Visit of Cardinal Wojytla; College joins Detroit Consortium of Catholic Colleges and Universities; lay students ad-

Date	POLAND	AMERICA/ UNITED STATES	POLISH AMERICA	POLISH SEMINARY/ ORCHARD LAKE SCHOOLS
				mitted to College and Seminary programs (women in 1970); Seminary graduates first person in permanent diaconate program
1970	Polish-West German treaty, recognizes Polish border on Odra-Nyssa rivers; worker strikes and riots bring about downfall of Gomulka; Edward Gierek elected party leader			*Pan z wami*, Polish missalette, begins publication
1971			John Cardinal Król chosen president of National Conference of Catholic Bishops	Construction of new Preparatory Residence; "Project: POLE"
1973		Oil embargo and economic inflation		Construction of Dombrowski Fieldhouse
1974		Resignation of President Nixon		Seminary authorized to grant master's degrees; Orchard Lake Ambassadors founded
1975		Communist victory in Vietnam; Helsinki Agreement and detente in Soviet-U.S. relations		

1976	Wave of strikes and protests brought under control; rise of political dissent		Visit of Cardinal Wojtyła and Polish bishops; College accredited by North Central Association
1977	Zbigniew Brzeziński appointed national security adviser to President Carter		Fr. Ziemba resigns and Fr. Stanley Milewski elected first Chancellor of the Schools; Seminary, College, and Preparatory receive separate administrative heads; Seminary introduces Master's of Religious Education program
			Chancellor's Senate founded
1978	Election of Karol Cardinal Wojtyła as Pope John Paul II		
1979	Visit of Pope John Paul II to Poland	Pope John Paul II visits Polish communities in U.S.	
1980	Strikes and shortages bring about downfall of Gierek; formation of Solidarity union		Expansion of College degree programs and majors with support of federal Title III grant
1981	Imposition of martial law; Solidarity underground	Conservative economic and social policies introduced by President Reagan	Major relief effort for Poland following martial law
1982	Unsuccessful assassination attempt on Pope John Paul II		

Date	POLAND	AMERICA/ UNITED STATES	POLISH AMERICA	POLISH SEMINARY/ ORCHARD LAKE SCHOOLS
1983	Formal end of martial law; continuing economic problems; Lech Wałęsa awarded Nobel Peace Prize			Reorganization and streamlining of Board of Regents; separate boards of control for each school
1985				Schools celebrate Centenary

INDEX

PERSONS, INSTITUTIONS, ORGANIZATIONS, AND PERIODICALS.

A
Alexander, C.S.S.F., Sr. M., 124
Alliance College, 41
Alliance of Lithuanian Roman Catholic Students of America, 38
Alumni Association, 37, 42, 82, 83, 118, 119, 141, 164
Alumnus, 82
Ambassadors, Orchard Lake, 142, 170
American Bishops War Relief Committee, 109
American Council of Polish Cultural Clubs, 153
American Federation of Labor, 161
Aniela, C.S.S.F. Sr., 81
Antochowski, Rev. Aloysius, 77
Aquinas Academy, 116, 168
Archives of Polonia and Orchard Lake, 143
Aristotle, 116
Assumption College, 40

B
Barabasz, Rev. Michael, 36, 44
Barski, Ignatius, 81
Barzyński, C.R., Rev. Vincent, 24, 43, 161

Black-Polish Conference, 145
Blejwas, Stanislaus, 151, 153
Bludgeon, 77
Board of Regents, 86, 140, 141, 172
Bociański, Andy, 79
Bójnowski, Rev. Lucjan, 120
Borgess, Bishop Caspar, 28, 33, 35, 45, 161
Bór-Komorowski, Tadeusz, 121
Boys from Poland, 109, 110, 119, 121, 167
Brooklyn, Roman Catholic Diocese of, 87
Brzeziński, Zbigniew, 171
Budnik, Peter, 39
Buffalo, Roman Catholic Diocese of, 87
Buhaczkowski, Rev. Witold, 36, 37, 40, 44-46, 55, 56, 62, 65-67, 69, 71, 163, 164
Buszek, Rev. John, 77

C
Campbell, Allen, 42
Campus Orchestra, 111, 121
Cendrowski, Rev. Alexander, 10, 77, 91, 110
Center for Pastoral Studies, 136, 169

Center for Polish Studies and Culture, 7, 143, 169
Chancellor's Senate, 142, 171
Chicago, Roman Catholic Archdiocese of, 87, 88
Chopcy z Polski (See: Boys from Poland)
Chrobot, Rev. Leonard, 10, 134, 145, 153
Ciechoradzki, Mr., 81
Ciszek, S.J., Rev. Walter, 105
College Choir, 111, 121
Columbus, Christopher, 156
Conference on Cultural Pluralism, 145
Congregation for the Propagation of the Faith, 45
Congregation of the Resurrection, 23-26, 43, 67
Congregation of the Sisters of St. Felix, 26, 28, 40, 42, 65, 81, 118, 124, 151, 160, 161, 166
Conrad Club, 116, 168
Conrad, Joseph, 117
Consortium of Catholic Colleges and Universities, 135, 169
Committee on Industrial Organization (C.I.O.), 166
Copeland, Joseph, T., 63
Copernicus, Nicolaus, 157
Council of Trent, 15, 36
Cyran, Rev. Constantine, 70, 91, 109
Czarnick, Raymond, 115
Częstochowa, Polish Shrine of, 15; Polish Shrine of American, 113

D
Dąbrowski Foundation, 119
Dąbrowski, Rev. Joseph, 10, 22-24, 26-28, 31-36, 38, 40, 42-46, 51, 65, 69, 70, 76, 106, 115, 119, 137, 147, 148, 152, 159, 160, 161, 163
Dearden, Archbishop John, 86, 114, 124
Democratic Party, 61, 166
Detroit, Roman Catholic Archdiocese of, 33, 70, 84-86, 111, 140, 167
Detroit Free Press, 152
Detroit News, 152
Dombrowski, Robert, 118
Dorothy, C.S.S.F., Sr., 81

E
Eagle (newspaper), 77, 153
Eagle (yearbook), 78, 117, 152, 166
Eucharistic League, 74, 164

F
Faculty War Relief for Poland, 109, 167
Ferry Seed Company, 29
Fidelitas Medal, 120, 124, 168
Filipowicz, Rev. Wallace, J., 113, 117, 124, 168, 169
Foley, Bishop John, 45
Ford Motor Company, 163
Friends of the Orchard Lake Schools, 110, 119, 141, 167

G
Gallagher, Bishop Michael, 45, 69, 70, 88, 92, 111
Geryk, Robert, 152
Gierek, Edward, 170, 171
Gierut, Rev. Joseph, 68, 111, 119, 152
Glaudel, John, 79
Głos Studenta (Student Voice), 41
Gmina Polska (Polish Commune), 160
Godrycz, Rev. John, 41, 46
Gomułka, Władysław, 168, 170
Górzelniaski, Francis, 55
Grabowski, Rev. Stanislaus, 91
Gregorian University, 46
Gribbs, Roman, 132
Grotto, Orchard Lake, 75, 76, 122, 123, 167
Grupa, Rev. Michael, 10, 62, 64, 66, 67, 69, 70, 82, 91, 115, 164, 165
Gutowski, John, 11

H
Hodur, Bishop Francis, 163
Homiletic and Pastoral Review, 153

I
Ireland, Archbishop John, 66

J
Jadwiga, Queen, 156
Jagiełło, King Władysław, 156
Jagiellonian University, 41, 156
Janicki, Rev. Stanislaus, 91
Jankowski, Joseph, 113, 114
Jański, C.R., Rev. Bogdan, 23
Jarecki, Rev. Leon, 36, 41
Jasiński, Rev. Valerius, 104-7, 110, 114, 116, 153
Jerzmanowski, Erasmus, 45
Jesus of Nazareth, 74, 113
John XXIII, Pope, 133
John Paul II, Pope, 125, 127, 144, 146-48, 169, 171
Juchniewicz, Jerry, 79

K

Kajsiewicz, C.R., Rev. Jerome, 23
Kant, Immanuel, 41
Kasprowicz, Rev. Francis, 119
Kłowo, Rev. Anthony, 65, 66, 74, 83, 91, 92, 111, 165, 166
Knights of Dąbrowski, 110, 169
Kolasiński, Rev. Dominik, 34, 35, 42, 43
Kosciński, Arthur, 86
Kosciuszko Foundation, 153, 163
Kościuszko, Thaddeus, 14, 158, 159
Kośnik, Rev. Anthony, 134
Kowalewski, Rev. Theodore, 80, 91
Kozdrój, Chester, 83
Kozłowski, Rev. Anthony, 162
Krawczyk, Rev. Edward, 91
Król, Archbishop John, 114, 170
Krych, Rev. Ladislaus, 91
Krzyżosiak, Rev. Ladislaus, 66, 67, 74, 83, 85, 86, 91, 92, 166, 167

L

Ladies Auxiliary of the Alumni Association, 83, 118, 141, 166
Lake Oracle, 77, 117
Lakeside Punch, 77
League of Nations, 164
Ledochowski, Archbishop Mieczysław, 16, 25, 48
Leo XIII, Pope, 25, 48, 49, 88, 161
Lincoln, Abraham, 160
Łobaza, Peter, 41, 91, 99, 109
Luchesia, C.S.S.F., Sr., 81

M

Machnikowski, Ignatius, 41, 91
Magnet, 74
Maksimik, Rev. Anthony, 91, 109
Malinowski, Rev. Leo, 79, 91
Martusiewicz, Andrew, 42, 91
Mazewski, Aloysius, 169
McKinley, William, 162
Metropolitan Clubs, 82, 164
Michigan: Board of Education, 85; Department of Education, 67; Superintendent of Education, 85
Michigan Military Academy, 40, 47, 61-63, 65, 163
Michigan-Ontario Collegiate Conference, 80
Mickiewicz, Adam, 159
Mieszko, Prince, 14, 156
Milewski, Rev. Stanley, 7, 10, 118, 127, 141, 171
Milinkiewicz, Rev. Boleslaus, 91
Miłosz, Czesław, 133
Mioduszewski, Rev. John, 83
Moczygemba, Rev. Leopold, 21, 24-26, 42, 48, 50, 88, 161
Moms and Dads Club, 113, 141
Moneta, Rev. John, 46
Mooney, Archbishop Edward, 68, 84-86, 92, 111
Mueller, Rev. John, 41, 45
Mueller, Rev. Francis, 40, 62
Mundelein, Archbishop G.W., 87
Muskie, Edmund, 146, 168

N

Napoleon, 18
National Catholic Education Association, 68
National Conference of Catholic Bishops, 134
National Democratic Party, 162
National Polish American-Jewish American Task Force, 145
Niedziela (Sunday), 41, 42, 44, 162
Nir, Rev. Roman, 11
Nixon, Richard M., 169, 170
North Central Assoc. of Colleges and Secondary Schools, 68-70, 112, 119, 136, 138, 152, 153, 170

O

O'Connell, Daniel, M., 152
Oldfather, C.H., 152, 153
Orlik, Rev. Francis, 74, 91, 115
Ostafin, Peter, 115

P

Pan z wami (The Lord be with You), 137, 170
Parot, Joseph, 151
Pastuch, Sam, 81
Peasants Party, 162
Pen and Inklings, 117
Phi Gamma Chi, 77, 78, 116, 165
Philadelphia, Roman Catholic Archdiocese of, 88
Piątkowski, Romuald, 41, 91
Piejda, Rev. Casimir, 119
Piłsudski, Josef, 164, 165
Piszek, Edward, 145, 146
Pittsburgh, Roman Catholic Diocese of, 87
Pius XII, Pope, 116
Piwowarski, Andrew, 41, 152
Plagens, Bishop Joseph, 92
Polish American Congress, 167
Polish American Historical Association, 7, 107, 115
Polish American Liturgical Center, 137, 169
Polish American Sports Hall of Fame, 144

Polish American Studies, 7, 107, 115, 116, 153
Polish Army in America, 164
Polish Homiletic Congress in America, 110
Polish Literary Society, 39, 75, 76, 115, 162
Polish National Alliance, 22, 26, 41-44, 83, 161
Polish National Catholic Church, 163
Polish Papal College, 23
Polish Review, 151
Polish Roman Catholic Association, 43
Polish Roman Catholic Union of America, 22, 25, 43, 83-85, 118, 161
Polish Socialist Party, 162
Polish Students Mission Society, 74, 164
Polish Union of the United States, 84, 85
Polish United Workers Party, 167
Polish Women's Alliance, 162
Pontiac Fire Department, 64
Pope John Paul II Center, 144, 169
Popielarz, Rev. Edward, 77, 78, 110, 116, 119
Prep Glee Club, 111, 121
Prep Laker, 117, 168
Pułaski, Casimir, 13, 158

R
Radzialowski, Thaddeus, 151, 152
Reagan, Ronald, 171
Renkiewicz, Frank, 7
Republican party, 162
Rhode, Bishop Paul, 44, 66, 163
Rogers, Joseph, 63
Roosevelt, Franklin, 112, 166
Rozmarek, Charles, 169
Różycki, Walter, 113
Rybiński, Rev. Joseph, 70, 74, 75, 91, 109
Rzeppa, Josephine, 75

S
Sacred Heart Seminary (Detroit), 111
St. Albertus Parish (Detroit), 28, 29, 33, 34, 40, 42, 47, 62
St. Aloysius Gonzaga, 75
St. Casimir, 37, 72, 76
St. Casimir Parish (Detroit), 34
St. Cecilia Club, 39
St. Francis of Assisi Parish (Detroit), 83
St. Hyacinth Parish (Detroit), 83
St. John's Seminary (Plymouth), 111

St. Joseph, 36, 72
St. Joseph's Seminary (Josephinum, Columbus), 45
St. Mary, 15, 53, 72, 74, 75, 83, 113, 114, 122, 123
St. Mary's College (Orchard Lake), 67-80, 85, 88, 111, 112, 114-17, 133-36, 138-41, 143, 152, 153, 165, 169, 171
St. Mary's Preparatory High School (Orchard Lake), 34-47, 63, 64, 67-80, 85, 88, 112, 113, 115, 135, 138-41, 143, 153, 168, 171
St. Mary's Seminary (Cincinnati), 111
St. Nicholas, 72
St. Stanislaus College (Weber High School), 67
St. Stanislaus, Bishop and Martyr, 156
St. Stanislaus Kostka, 36, 75
St. Stanislaus Kostka Parish (Chicago), 161
St. Stanislaus Kostka Society, 160
St. Thomas Aquinas, 116, 117
SS. Cyril and Methodius, 33, 34, 116
SS. Cyril and Methodius Apostolate, 116
SS. Cyril and Methodius Seminary, 33-47, 61-89, 109-12, 114, 115, 133, 134, 136-41, 143, 152, 153, 170, 171
Schemanske, Frank, 86
Schola Cantorum, 111, 120
Schwitalla, Alphonse M., 152, 153
Seets, Gene, 127
Semenenko, C.R., Rev. Peter, 23, 24
Seminary Orchestra-Band, 39, 55, 76
Siemiradzki, Thomas, 14, 44
Skarga Society, 116, 168
Skarga, Peter, 76, 117
Skrocki, Rev. Edward, 78, 115
Slavsky, John, 119
Slavsky, Robert, 119
Słowo i Liturgia (The Word and the Liturgy), 137
Sobieski, King John, 157
Society of Christ, 108
Society of Jesus, 40, 66
Society of the Sacred Heart, 36, 74
Sodalis, 75, 82, 115, 152, 164
Sodality of the Immaculate Conception, 75, 164
Solidarity, 133, 171
Stefan, Bruno, 115
Stein, Leo, 145
Strauss, Joseph, 39
Stungis, Stan, 79
Surge, 117

Swastek, Rev. Joseph, 106, 109, 115, 151-53
Sweetest Heart of Mary Parish (Detroit), 42
Świeczkowska, Clara, 75
Świetlik, Francis, 103
Syski, Rev. Alexander, 152
Szulak, S.J., Rev. Francis, 36
Szumal, Rev. Edward, 92, 105, 109, 121, 167, 168

T
Tenerowicz, Rev. Stanislaus, 91
Teutonic Knights, 14, 156

U
United Automobile Workers of America, 61
United States Postal Service, 63, 168
United States Supreme Court, 168
University of Detroit, 40, 66, 79, 136
University of Kraków (See: Jagiellonian University)
University of Lublin, Catholic, 125
University of Michigan, 67
University of Warsaw, 22

V
Van Deusen, Clarence, 114
Vashak (Washak), Walter, 86
Vatican, 17
Vatican Council II, 133, 136, 144

W
Wajda, Edward, 110
Wałęsa, Lech, 133, 172
Waraksa, Rev. Henry, 111, 121
Waszyca, Rev. Arnold, 64, 75
Weber, Joseph, 42
Węgier, Rev. Francis, 91
Wójnicki, Bishop Stephen, 83, 85, 166
Wojtusiak, Rev. Michael, 91
Wojtyła, Karol Cardinal (See: John Paul II)
Wotta, Rev. Andrew, 79, 91, 102, 109
Wrzos (Heather), 76
Wyspiański, Stanisław, 148

Z
Żądała, Rev. Adalbert, 92
Zaleski, Bishop Alexander, 114
Zasucha, John, 81
Ziemba, Rev. Walter, 10, 115, 116, 119, 125, 134, 140, 141, 145, 146, 153, 169, 171
Żiółkowski, C.S.S.F., Sr. M. Janice, 151
Zgoda (Harmony), 41, 44
Zmysłowski, Clemens, 81
Żychowicz, Andrzej, 81